MW00606682

Shingle Style

Shingle Style

Living in San Francisco's Brown Shingles

Lucia Howard | David Weingarten

Foreword
Daniel P. Gregory

Photography
David Duncan Livingston

RIZZOLI
NEW YORK

New York · Paris · London · Milan

Table of Contents

28
Polk/Williams House
San Francisco, 1892

36
Carrigan House
San Anselmo, 1892

70
Flagg House
Berkeley, 1901

76
Gregory House
Berkeley, 1904

108
Van Sant House
Berkeley, 1906

116
Senger House
Berkeley, 1906

148
Thorsen House
Berkeley, 1909

156
Blake House
Berkeley, 1911

46

Churchill House

Napa, 1892

54

Siegriest House

Oakland, 1900

62

Waybur House

San Francisco, 1901

84

Kofoid House

Berkeley, 1905

92

McHenry House

Piedmont, 1905

100

Tufts House

San Anselmo, 1906

124

James House

Berkeley, 1908

132

Kellogg House

Berkeley, 1908

140

Tibbetts House

Berkeley, 1909

164

Dungan House

Berkeley, 1912

172

Adams/Dodd House

Berkeley, 1913

180

The Igloo

San Anselmo, 1913

Foreword

Daniel P. Gregory

Many years ago, I attended a festive lunch in San Francisco to celebrate the wedding of close friends. It was at a house on Pacific Avenue in Presidio Heights, and on my plate was an unusual party favor: a long, tapered, slightly torqued, burnt-toast-hued redwood shingle tied at the middle with a bright green satin ribbon. Our innovative hostess knew it would appeal— she had salvaged it from the discard woodpile at a neighbor's house under restoration. And so I found myself holding a piece of Bay Area architectural history: a fragment of Bernard Maybeck's famously animistic Goslinski House of 1909, an exemplar of the Bay Area Shingle Style.

Now, looking back, and with Lucia Howard and David Weingarten's superb book on the houses of this era as a guide, I can see the DNA of Bay Region architecture more clearly. Building on the work of scholars like John Beach, David Gebhard, Esther McCoy, Richard Longstreth, and Sally Woodbridge, Lucia and David have zeroed in on an important gene pool. For these are the houses that influenced later Bay Region modern architects like William Wurster and Gardner Dailey— not to mention Joe Esherick, whose marvelous Hedgerow House is represented in this book—in the development of an architecture that, according to the great critic Lewis Mumford, writing in the catalogue to an exhibit on Bay Area architecture in 1949, "though it was thoroughly modern...was not tied to the tags and clichés of the so-called International Style."[1]

In that same catalogue, Wurster recalled his first experience as a freshman architecture student at Berkeley in 1913, when he attended an evening gathering in the redwood-framed Rieber House of 1904 by Coxhead & Coxhead: "It was a big room with four-foot-wide boards in panel form on the walls and ceiling. The redwood was left unfinished as it came from the tree, which takes on a pink-brown color with the years. A natural pine floor, no carpets or rugs and a fireplace with a raised hearth used for a seat the twenty-four feet of the width of the room...It took great skill to bring about this room. It meant giving up the idea of windows as holes in the wall, of competing with the view with the triviality of fabric, color, or pattern. It meant steering free of the ruffles of existence. The gain was rewarding, for I know that many were inspired, and you find it in the work of Schweinfurth, Coxhead, the Greenes, Polk, Howard, and Maybeck."[2] Wurster studied in the School of Architecture building designed by John Galen Howard and known as the "Ark," itself a modest but iconic redwood structure covered with shingles inside and out.

Wurster was so taken with works by the previous architectural generation that in 1952 he and his wife Catherine Bauer purchased the barnlike brown shingle house on Greenwood Terrace in north Berkeley that Howard had designed for Warren and Sadie Gregory (my grandparents) in 1904; the house is included in this book. Wurster had visited it often as a college friend of the Gregorys' older son, Don (and had subsequently designed the Gregory Farmhouse at Santa Cruz, for Sadie, in 1927). It was Sadie who sold Wurster the Berkeley house. Wurster only added French doors to the living room and simplified the garden with a gravel terrace. The Wursters, who ultimately cofounded U.C. Berkeley's College of Environmental Design, entertained faculty members, students, and guest lecturers there often. I can remember visiting them as a boy with my parents and meeting Lewis Mumford in the living room. White rugs, Aalto furniture, and modern paintings and artwork by Gyorgy Kepes and Adaline Kent stood out against the dark redwood board-and-batten walls and clinker brick fireplace. It was spare and elegant, modern and traditional all at the same time.

So what is it about Brown Shingles that made them so popular? The redwood was plentiful, and as Fred T. Hodgson wrote in the preface to his *Practical Bungalows and Cottages for Town and Country* pattern book of 1906, "the redwood shingles and shakes used on the coast have a pleasanter and warmer coloring than cedar shingles whether stained or not."[3] They were durable and relatively rot-resistant. And finally, shingles suited a light wood-frame construction and could cover large areas inexpensively and plainly or as a textured foil for more exuberant ornament. In short, shingles, and by extension the Bay Area Shingle Style, offered architects flexibility and the freedom to invent without abandoning architectural precedent. And they offered a medium for what Mumford called "a steady organic growth."

That Maybeck shingle and the houses in this book are genetic talismans. They cover—or perhaps I should say unravel—an important strand in the evolving history of Bay Area architecture. Redwood—an architectural nucleotide—rides again.

7

Introduction

SHINGLED HOME ADORNED WITH VINES.

NEW ZEALAND MAORI HOUSE SHOWING ROOF OF MODERATE PITCH.

Top "Shingle Home Adorned with Vines," from *The Simple Home* by Charles Keeler. Keeler's manifesto leads with this image of the 1893 Sarah Goodrich House in Berkeley (architect unknown), exemplifying his belief that Brown Shingle gardens should be thought of as "nature controlled by art."

Above "New Zealand Maori House Showing Roof of Moderate Pitch," from *The Simple Home* by Charles Keeler. Keeler, fascinated by exotic buildings, employed examples of "savage architecture" to illustrate his ideas.

I. East Coast/West Coast

Right Coast/Left Coast

Known in the Bay Area with considerable affection as Brown Shingles, the dark, redwood shingle-swathed buildings of the late nineteenth and early twentieth centuries embody a signal period in the region's history. Set within lush gardens, alongside and occasionally across brooks and streams, planned around and complementing their sites' topographies and landscapes, made of natural materials, Brown Shingles gave architectural form to distinctively Bay Area social values in the realms of nature, art, and freedoms of all types. These identical values fueled a range of local movements over the course of a century, from the Sierra Club to the Summer of Love, and gave rise to diverse characters, from John Muir to Allen Ginsberg.

In Berkeley, especially, where shingled houses, churches, and institutional buildings surround the campus of the great university and hold their ground alongside a dense hodgepodge of later buildings, the Brown Shingles embody the legacy of the early naturalist intellectuals who during the late nineteenth and early twentieth centuries set out the relationship between this place and ways of living within it. Living, working, learning, meeting, and praying in redwood-sheathed Brown Shingles, set in the midst of a dense, left coast Edenic landscape, was at once reality and metaphor—a modern, artistic life inhabiting the redwood trees of the ancient, primeval forest.

Is There a Bay Area Shingle Style?

The Bay Area's Brown Shingles are connected less by a specific style than by a peculiarly Northern Californian set of beliefs. "The Bay Area Tradition (which includes the Brown Shingles) represents not a style, but a process of synthesis and transformation: a design approach with trademarks and no rules," explains John Beach in *Bay Area Houses* (1974). Though difficult to define, these "trademarks" make the Brown Shingles' design approach easy to recognize.

Many of the architects included here arrived in San Francisco within a few years of one another, in the late 1880s. Though still a young city, San Francisco was already the nation's seventh largest. The Bay Area's physical beauty, economic vitality, mild climate, and social tolerance lured these ambitious and talented young men from across the United States and Europe at the conclusion of their training in the leading architectural offices of the East Coast, England, and France.

McKim, Mead & White, Isaac Bell House, Newport, Rhode Island, 1883. Courtesy the Historic American Buildings Survey, Library of Congress, Prints & Photographs Division. The Bell House is a highly sophisticated East Coast Shingle Style dwelling, with extensive porches and paradigmatic, bold, vernacularly referenced forms.

The promise and romance of California, coupled with its physical and social distance from the middle-class establishment, attracted those seeking freedom in architecture as well as in life. "A nearly legendary California was created, an idyllic land where anything was possible and where the rules of conventional society did not necessarily apply," writes Beach. "It was a place where man's mark on the environment demanded the emphatic, the extravagant, the fabulous."

Architecture was only one of the arts calling people west. During this period, Berkeley had more poets than any other town in the country, according to *Berkeley Bohemia*, abounding with poets' publications, dinners, and clubs. With poets, painters, and professors as clients, architects were given license to experiment with almost everything. Buildings were unique and eccentric, providing for a life integrated with both art and nature, yet often filled with whimsy and drama. Taking a range of forms, buildings were attuned to the varieties of topography, microclimate, and unusual lot configuration. Architectural elements and styles from multiple sources and eras were often employed simultaneously, fueling the development of the Bay Area's singular eclecticism.

Charles Keeler—poet, naturalist, and ardent and articulate advocate of an approach to architecture closely integrated with nature—outlined a comprehensive set of ideas about how to design and live in the Bay Area in his 1904 manifesto *The Simple Home*. Including details down to window coverings, furnishings, and tableware, Keeler enthusiastically laid out the Brown Shingle's central design philosophies. Speaking for others who, like him, had abondoned rigid middle-class, late-Victorian worlds for the freedom of California, Keeler avowed, "A life hedged in with formality is like a plant stifled by surrounding weeds."

Keeler envisioned the home as a "family temple" whose design had a spiritual mission, which could only be realized through Art. "We must demand of our architect that he be a real creative artist" because "the building of houses is an art, not a trade." Elaborating on his ideas of building in materials and forms particular to place, Keeler included examples of Thai temples and Polynesian huts, reflecting a fascination with exoticism that infused the architecture he espoused. Keeler viewed the phenomenon of developer-built housing with disgust: "The real estate agent and the investor confer, and as a result we have rows of houses put up to sell to shiftless home seekers who are too indifferent to think out their own needs, and helpless take what has been built for the trade." Were Keeler writing today, imagine his contempt.

For a quarter-century, from approximately 1890 to the mid-1910s, redwood shingles sheathed buildings of every style and type—medieval cottages and Swiss chalets; houses designed like cabins, palaces, and barns; dwellings inspired by Japanese temples and Georgian town houses. The Vedanta Society's multi-domed temple in San Francisco, which survived the 1906 earthquake, embodies the spirit of amalgamation animating architectural design at the time. According to a pamphlet published by Swami Trigunatita in 1906, "This temple may be considered as a combination of a Hindu temple, a Christian church, a Mohammedan mosque, a Hindu math or monastery, and an American residence." Neighborhoods of (developer-built) Brown Shingles sprang up, especially in Berkeley, with clusters of similarly designed houses and churches all around San Francisco Bay as well as in distant California towns where Bay Area residents moved or summered. Redwood shingles bound these buildings together into a cohesive extended architectural family, lending them a simplified rustic appearance, yet with enormous diversity and eccentricity.

East Coast Shingle Style
In his 1955 work, *The Shingle Style: Architectural Theory and Design from Richardson to the Origins of Wright*, which has influenced generations of architects and architectural historians, Yale professor Vincent Scully named and precisely characterized the Shingle Style as a defining moment in American architecture. In the hands of a group of talented Boston and New York architects, a distinctly American style of domestic architecture evolved from the Queen Anne and Stick styles, typifying American domestic architecture in the latter half of the nineteenth century. "[T]he American house had now undergone a variety of changes adapting it to American conditions, functional requirements, and materials," wrote Scully. "The openness and flow of space are American, so are the sheltering void of the piazza, the lightly scaled woodwork, and the rough shingles."

Characteristically employed for seaside and summer houses where rustic simplicity complemented a leisurely, informal life away from crowded cities, these houses were often large, occasionally immense. Unpainted shingle cladding referred to American colonial architecture, said Scully, to deliberately create "the

insistent suburban evocation of a lost agrarian simplicity…directly related to the simplified life of the shore or the suburb." These houses were intended as idylls in both design and function, conjuring a link to a mythological American past.

Forty years after Scully defined the Shingle Style, American architectural historian Leland Roth, in *Shingle Styles: Innovation and Tradition in American Architecture 1874 to 1982* (1999), revisited the phenomenon, including examples built after publication of Scully's book. "So the Shingle Style emerged, called into being by the leisured classes, who desired an architecture that spoke of easy and carefree pastimes, an architecture that wasn't pretentious or boastful, that connected with an ancestral past but was not held in check by it," explained Roth. "It was an architecture of fresh spirit and unbridled expansiveness that stood in sharp contrast to the buildings of the *nouveaux riches* dazzled by Old World traditions and hierarchies." Shingle Style house clients were people of taste and means, who eschewed some, though hardly all, ostentation (remember that many of these "modest" houses nonetheless contained dozens of rooms).

Architecturally, the East Coast Shingle Style employed a set of stylistic vocabularies featuring primarily simplified Queen Anne, Tudor or Jacobean, medieval English vernacular, and American Colonial vernacular forms, and a form Roth describes as the "triangular gable." The various parts might be deployed picturesquely or simplified to one large shape. Extravagant exterior decorative woodwork, characterizing the earlier Queen Anne and Stick styles, gave way to continuous shingled surfaces sporting occasional swells and flares, with simplified detailing around openings and eaves. Separate public rooms at interiors were merged into continuous flowing spaces, divided by screens and partial walls, and often oriented to a large "living hall."

During the building boom of the 1870s and 1880s, this radically new approach to residential design spread along the northern East Coast and as far west as Chicago. Published extensively in *American Architect* magazine, the great houses of the East Coast Shingle Style and their somewhat more modest suburban cousins influenced architects across the United States as well as in Europe. Beginning in the late 1880s, this intensely creative and uniquely American impulse in the country's architectural history lost steam and was overtaken by a European-based eclecticism. Yet as reported by Roth as well as by Scully, in *The Shingle Style Today, or The*

William Keith, *Reverend Joseph Worcester's House*. Collection of Richard Pettler and Wanda Westberg, Berkeley, California. Worcester and the great landscape painter William Keith, naturalist John Muir's close friend, depicted Worcester's 1872 cabin many times, contributing to its influence on an entire generation of architects in San Francisco.

Historian's Revenge (1974), it has reappeared in some recent buildings and has been embraced by a new generation of architects, acquiring new, particularly American symbolic and cultural significances.

Bay Area Shingle Style

East Coast Shingle Style houses of the late nineteenth century were very often country houses and summer retreats built for the well-to-do and gotten up, more or less demurely, in period architectural finery. The period's West Coast shingle houses, on the other hand, were year-round places, often designed for the Bay Area's intellectual avant-garde—artists, writers, and religious leaders, as well as the occasional architect—and designed to reflect a substantial measure of bohemian rusticity, eschewing finery. Rather than escaping from the crowded and polluted cities to shingled houses and badminton lawns, Californians relaxed and vacationed by camping and hiking. Being in nature, living much of life out-of-doors, held spiritual and emotional meaning given ideal expression in primitive-appearing, rustic architecture.

The tallest, most ancient trees on earth—hundreds, sometimes thousands of years old—coast redwoods, or California redwoods, grow only in the narrow strip of land along the Northern California coast, extending into southern Oregon. Sacred to indigenous people, as well as some later inhabitants, these redwood groves inspired a regional reverence for nature. Iconic and majestic, the trees also had great commercial utility, providing material for the late-nineteenth- and early-twentieth-century building boom in Northern California. While cutting and milling old-growth redwood is now considered unconscionable, in the nineteenth century, cladding buildings in unpainted redwood shingles linked them visually and symbolically to the natural world.

Bay Area house clients were not necessarily well-to-do. Architects and many early clients styled themselves "bohemians," some of whom joined together in 1892 to form the Bohemian Club in San Francisco, initially a group of journalists, architects, and artists who met regularly for cultural evenings. According to founding member and poet George Sterling, "There are two elements, at least, that are essential to Bohemianism. The first is devotion or addiction to one or more of the Seven Arts: the other is poverty." Commissioned by this impecunious clientele, Bay Area Brown Shingles were only rarely outsized, with many built on the most difficult, and therefore least expensive, sites.

Architectural Sources

Though shingled houses on both coasts can be seen in part as an American reinvention of ideas informing the English Arts and Crafts movement, Bay Area Brown Shingles have a distinctly regional source. In 1876, a Swedenborgian minister named Joseph Worcester designed and began building an iconic redwood cabin, highly picturesque and low to the ground with a craggy, irregular profile, shingled exterior, and redwood paneled interior, in the town of Piedmont, in the East Bay region on San Francisco Bay. Paintings of the cabin by Worcester's close friend William Keith, the great California landscape painter, ensured the cabin's influence spread well beyond Worcester's immediate circle. Though Worcester built another shingled home on San Francisco's Russian Hill in 1883, he continued to visit the small cabin. The place figured prominently in the Bay Area's cultural history: Jack London penned *The Call of the Wild* while staying there from 1903 to 1905, according to Leslie Freudenheim in *Building with Nature* (1974), and Bernard Maybeck lived next door for a year in 1890.

Though Worcester's cabin appeared simple, an outgrowth of the local vernacular, it was, in fact, also an intellectual exercise, explicitly reflecting the pastor's beliefs in the spiritual and healthful importance of Nature and in the moral power of Art. Worcester grew up in Boston, attended Harvard, and maintained a close friendship throughout his life with the great Chicago architect Daniel Burnham. Charismatic and energetic, Worcester was also a devoted student of architecture. He was familiar with East Coast architects' explorations of colonial vernacular architecture, as well as the writings of architectural theorist John Ruskin and designer William Morris, who is often credited with establishing the Arts and Crafts movement in England.

Familiar histories of the Shingle Style include examples in the San Francisco Bay Area only as a footnote, with houses labeled Arts and Crafts seen as poor country cousins to the great, high-style East Coast shingled dwellings. The heyday of the Bay Area's Brown Shingle period awaited the arrival of Charles Keeler in 1887, and, two years later, of Ernest Coxhead, Willis Polk, and Bernard Maybeck, architects well versed in the Shingle Style. Still, the redwood-shingled Worcester cottage in Piedmont predates the golden age of the East Coast Shingle Style, which Scully dates from 1878 to 1882, and exemplifies the very different motives and purposes of the Bay Area Shingle Style in comparison to its more dandified East Coast counterparts. Though San Francisco's architects freely adopted and reimagined elements of the Shingle Style vocabulary, the resemblances were often matters of form rather than content. Deceptively simple, with a primitive and rustic profile that belies its sophistication and intellectual expressiveness, Worcester's cabin is the real progenitor of the Bay Area Shingle Style, predating its right coast cousins.

The Difference in Design
Though the bicoastal family resemblance is strong, the Bay Area Brown Shingles shelter a very different type of resident from an environment bearing little resemblance to that of the East Coast. San Francisco's physical beauty—the dramatic coastline, expansive vistas of hills and Bay, magnificent natural landscape—is its most familiar, most photogenic attraction. Yet an equal glory is the place's climate. Temperate year-round, with no rain for months during the summer (resulting in a near absence of tiny biting creatures), its Mediterranean climate makes the Bay Area among the most livable places in the United States, while on the East Coast, home to many of the grandest Shingle Style houses, even by the sea summers range from hot and humid to very hot and dripping wet. This Eastern climate led to the popularity of one of that style's characteristic design devices, the wide, deep wraparound porch. These great porches and verandahs do double duty, providing cool, shady places to be outdoors and protecting and shading the interiors. Bay Area shingle houses rarely include substantial porches on the main level, though many feature covered sleeping porches off upstairs bedrooms; sleeping outdoors was widely believed to be conducive to good health. Large windows, often with no shading, capture views and let in warmth on those days when fogs create a chill.

At the interior, Bay Area Brown Shingles often possess decidedly eccentric plans, with surprising spatial sequences and complex wood-paneled stairs that seem outsized compared to the rooms they reach. Unlike their East Coast cousins, Bay Area shingle house plans make much of changes in level, opening to distant views, often turning and changing shape and focus, choreographing a sequence through many rooms. These very original plans and arrangements were often designed for elaborate "entertainments."

Bay Area Brown Shingle architects worked with programs and budgets much smaller than their East Coast counterparts yet made dwellings which are architecturally dense. "Coxhead, Polk, and Maybeck often used a rich assortment of elements set at a tiny scale, and compacted them into small buildings," remarked architectural historian John Beach.

These architects manipulated scale both up and down; ornament was often oversized, while other elements were made miniature. Schooled in an eclectic design tradition that specified correct proportions, they gleefully broke almost every rule, distorting expected relationships. After all, they were bohemians! These buildings are filled with what Beach describes as "playful outrages against correct taste." While the Shingle Style unleashed the dogs of invention, Bay Area architects ran those dogs in many directions, experimenting with form and program, color and ornament, structure and materials.

II. Ernest

The history of architecture arriving in San Francisco very often begins in the 1890s and is almost always told as something out of Joseph Conrad's *Heart of Darkness*. Highly trained architects, including Bernard Maybeck, Willis Polk, and Ernest Coxhead (all of whose work features prominently in this volume), make their ways from civilization's centers, across oceans and wild terrain, finally arriving in the foreboding, rough-and-ready, cultural backwater that is San Francisco. Here, despite their talent and refined abilities, these architects' sensibilities are soon affected by the place's bohemianism, radical freethinking, and general errancy. In this frontier city, so the story goes, beyond the reach of high culture and intellectual rigor, rational hardheadedness dissolves, and caprice, and sometimes chaos, rush in to fill the void.

While the consequences of this environment were not Kurtzian malignity, they were, at least in terms of modern architectural history, nearly as suspect—eclectic, highly idiosyncratic, and inventive buildings, reflective of eccentric, evanescent local temperament, as opposed to the era's agreed-upon civilized, academic norms.

This Conradian, more than a little condescending model of San Francisco's architectural history is remarkably pervasive and enduring. Late-nineteenth- and early-twentieth-century American architecture journals, for example, trivialized Bernard Maybeck's highly atmospheric buildings while speculating on his bohemian ways.

More recently, in 1983, an otherwise excellent MIT Press history of the period, *On the Edge of the World: Four Architects in San Francisco at the Turn of the Century*, repeats these old patterns.

Of the volume's "four architects"—Ernest Coxhead, Willis Polk, A. C. Schweinfurth, and Bernard Maybeck—Polk and especially Maybeck are better known, though it might be argued that Coxhead's work was the most influential. Maybeck acknowledged this debt; Polk worked for him.

As John Beach observed in *Bay Area Houses*, Coxhead's eclecticism worked in ways far different than that of lesser designers, whose "operative attitude...is that an architectural style is a design mode rather than a design resource." Beach describes the architect's best known San Francisco house this way:

Top Ernest Coxhead, San Francisco, c. 1905. Courtesy Mary Ann Beach and Richard Longstreth

Above Coxhead and Coxhead, Church of St. John the Evangelist, San Francisco, 1890–91, destroyed in the 1906 earthquake and fire. Courtesy Mary Ann Beach and Richard Longstreth. With its imposing, eccentric pyramidal roof rising out of a crowd of smaller shingled forms, this building was nicknamed "St. Roofus."

14

[T]he 1902 Waybur House is Coxhead at his most playful. Above a squat, heavily pedimented entrance, the treads and risers of the circulation stair are pulled through the facade, distorting, in a mannerist fashion, the expected form of the Palladian window which lights the stair hall...Coxhead uses the vernacular element (large areas of unbroken shingle wall) as a backdrop against which various design elements (Georgian details manipulated in unorthodox ways; giant windows for light and views; unexpected contrasts of scale) create a complex series of cultural and esthetic cross references. Palladio and mannerism, the vernacular and Georgian—pushed and pulled, distorted and made unexpected.

This robust intersection of multiple architectural styles, surprising shifts of scale, and upset of the expected, together with idiosyncratic, picturesque planning and building massing, are at the heart of Coxhead's best work from the 1890s to the early 1900s.

These buildings are precursors to Maybeck's later, even more determinedly Romantic and eclectic buildings from the 1900s onward. He writes, in *Palace of Fine Arts and Lagoon* (1915), of his approach to the design of his best known building, "the process is similar to that of matching the color of ribbons. You just pick up a blue ribbon, hold it alongside the sample in your hand, and at a glance you know it matches, or does not. You do the same with architecture; you examine a historic form and see whether the effect it produced in your mind matches the feeling you are trying to portray." While Maybeck and later architects built upon and eventually outshone Coxhead's eclecticism, none exceeded his dexterity with the simple redwood shingle.

In 1963, architect Louis Kahn famously interviewed a brick: "'What do you want Brick?' And Brick says to you

'I like an Arch,'" wrote Kahn. Imagine Ernest Coxhead conducting a similar interview with a redwood shingle. In his hands, shingles formed arches both classical and Gothic; they sheathed buildings styled Palladian and Georgian and Byzantine, as we've seen, as well as medieval, Arts and Crafts, and, of course, Shingle Style; they made walls and roofs, buttresses and ornament; they slid over surfaces, gathered around openings, seemed stretched taut across some walls while loosely draped over others; they were plain and patterned, large and small and very small, the perfect foil and the main event. With this simplest, slightest of building materials, Coxhead was a master prestidigitator.

Coxhead's architectural dexterity developed early on. Born in 1863 in Eastbourne, East Sussex, England, he was articled to a local civil engineer at age fifteen. By 1883, he reached London, where he was employed by an architect and, in the same year, gained admission to the Royal Academy of Arts. In 1886, the apparently ambitious young man was elected an associate of the Royal Institute of British Architects and soon awarded an RIBA silver medal.

The following year, relying on the promise of work from the Episcopal Diocese of Los Angeles, Ernest, along with his brother Almeric, set sail for California, a further measure of the young architect's drive. From 1887 through 1889, Ernest and Almeric designed the majority of Episcopal churches in Southern California. With the waning of the building boom in Los Angeles, the brothers left for San Francisco in 1889, again following the prospect of church commissions, as well as the possibilities of work in a more affluent city. Their office was small, generally employing just two or three draftsmen, but work was steady, and the projects they realized were increasingly distinctive.

15

Coxhead and Coxhead, Ernest and Almeric Coxhead House (left), 1893, and McGauley House (right), 1892, San Francisco. Courtesy Mary Ann Beach and Richard Longstreth. Entry to Coxhead's own exceedingly picturesque house is halfway along the side it shares with a dwelling the firm designed a year earlier.

Among these were the large, remarkable, thoroughly eclectic St. John the Evangelist in San Francisco and the much smaller, though even more idiosyncratic and picturesque, Chapel of St. John the Evangelist in Monterey. As Richard Longstreth observes in *On the Edge of the World*, "By 1893 an important shift occurred in Coxhead's approach." Some of this, undoubtedly, had to do with the end of his work for the Episcopal Church. After 1892, he designed no more churches for the client who had sustained the firm over the previous five years, a turn that must have been both alarming and liberating.

Just as important, Coxhead came into the sphere of Joseph Worcester, the San Francisco Swedenborgian minister whose circle included naturalist John Muir, painter William Keith, and architects Bernard Maybeck and Willis Polk, among many others possessed of artistic temperament. Emanuel Swedenborg is described by the *Encyclopedia of Religion* as a "Swedish scientist and mystic" who lived from 1688 to 1772 and was interested in formulating a scientific understanding of creation. His noteworthy career as an inventor and scientist was upended on Easter, 1744, when he commenced having prophetic dreams and visions. A consequence of this was Swedenborg's claim that God had directed him to reform Christianity and arranged for him to visit heaven and hell, where he spoke with angels and demons. In 1758, he wrote that the Last

Judgment had occurred the previous year. Joseph Worcester, born in Boston in 1836, was a third-generation Swedenborgian minister in the Church of the New Jerusalem. Influenced by Emerson and Wordsworth, Worcester "viewed the material world as a manifestation of God," as William Kostura writes in *Russian Hill*. Too constrained by life in Massachusetts, he made his way to San Francisco in 1867. By 1870, his congregation was meeting in a San Francisco auditorium known as Druid's Hall.

Worcester was also a largely self-taught architect who designed several modest, though highly influential, houses for himself and for friends. This provided the minister with substantial common ground with Coxhead and other architects. One can imagine that Coxhead's open-minded Episcopalianism neatly met Worcester's divine naturalism.

During this period, Coxhead's work, very largely residential, veered toward an increasingly outspoken eclecticism, toward massing increasingly picturesque, and toward planning more attuned to the site and its particulars. A result is that Coxhead is often misunderstood as an Arts and Crafts architect. In fact, as historian John Beach reminds us, Arts and Crafts was a resource for Coxhead, one of many for this most original architect, a means rather than an end.

Coxhead and Coxhead, Charles Murdoch House, San Francisco, 1893. Courtesy Mary Ann Beach and Richard Longstreth. The house's plain shingled wall flares over the street entry, while on the street facade's left, an eccentric offset dormer is paired with a large bay window below.

Beginning in the first decade of the new century, with rising enthusiasm among the well-to-do for more lavish houses, Coxhead's opportunities diminished. Affluent clients wanted Italian palazzi and classical temples, not redwood-shingled cottages. Coxhead attempted to adjust to the shift in style, turning out houses more classically inspired. Interestingly, though, for an architect whose ambition had once propelled him to the edge of the world, his heart seems not to have been in the new work, which became somewhat pedestrian. In part, this may have been a consequence of the death in 1905 of his wife, Helen, while she gave birth to the couple's third child. When Almeric died in 1928, Ernest continued the firm on his own. Longstreth recounts that Ernest "was seventy when he died in 1933, forgotten by most of his colleagues and having passed his prime more than a quarter-century earlier."

The decline in Coxhead's commissions in the face of changing architectural styles is part of a pattern seen repeatedly in Bay Area architectural history. With increasing means, the region's well-to-do have often turned to designers producing more up-to-date and expensive-looking buildings. Beginning early in the twentieth century, those in San Francisco who could afford it imported East Coast and European architects for especially ambitious projects, a practice that continues today. Ironically, though, the most important, most memorable Bay Area places have always been designed by Bay Area architects like Ernest Coxhead.

III. Brown Shingle Culture

Environmentalists
At age twenty-nine, John Muir was blinded in an industrial accident at a factory in Indianapolis. When his sight returned several months later, he changed his life's course and planned a "thousand-mile walk," taking him to Florida, Cuba, and the Amazon. Surviving illness and a variety of dangerous encounters, he reached Cuba. The availability of a boat to San Francisco, rather than South America, in conjunction with his weakness from severe bouts of malaria, caused a change in Muir's plans. His wanderlust undimmed by illness and misadventure, Muir set off for Yosemite a few days after reaching San Francisco in 1869.

Muir was a passionate naturalist in an age when the discipline was coming into its own. Explorations undertaken by scientists gained fame, and intense interest in the subject led Charles Darwin, despite a tendency

17

Top William H. Seward Tree with Galen Clark cabin, Mariposa Giant Sequoia Grove, Yosemite, 1872, by Eadweard Muybridge. The simple, tiny redwood cabin just beyond this colossal tree was similar to John Muir's Hangnest, built a year earlier along Yosemite Falls. Courtesy the Bancroft Library, University of California at Berkeley, California

Center J. L. Barker, a pioneer settler in Berkeley, at his summer house in the Santa Cruz mountains, c. 1910. Tree trunks and beams form the porch, while a densely planted trellised walk leads to the garden. Courtesy the Berkeley Architectural Heritage Association and the Barker Family

Above Temple of the Wings interior, with Mrs. Boynton, right, and her daughter Sulgwynn, left. Florence Boynton dressed her children in free-flowing robes and spent her days in the open-air Temple of the Wings, in the heart of Berkeley's Nut Hill, across from Maybeck's own house. Courtesy the Berkeley Architectural Heritage Association

to seasickness, to undertake a five-year voyage aboard the *Beagle* (though he traveled hundreds of miles by foot and on horse rather than remaining aboard as the ship encountered constant rough weather). The African adventures of David Livingstone began with his first expedition in 1840 and concluded when he was "discovered" by H. M. Stanley in 1871. For Muir, recovering from malaria, Yosemite appeared almost as a vision. He stayed for two years and experienced in the place transcendent power, describing it in a letter as "nature's temple," a phrase later used as the title of a collection of Muir's writing. While employed at the hotel in Yosemite Valley owned by the Hutchings family, Muir constructed his "Hangnest," a log cabin where he slept in a hammock over a stream but under a roof. More like a carefully arranged campsite with walls than a house, Muir's Hangnest prefigures Joseph Worcester's Piedmont cabin, constructed a few years later. It is likely that Worcester may have seen the Hangnest when he visited the hotel during this period.

The Hangnest took the constituent elements of the forest and condensed them into a hypernatural place. The desire to concentrate the experience of nature, to rearrange elements from the forest into buildings that seem a part of nature, inspires the Bay Area Brown Shingles. Built over creeks, using redwood logs and granite boulders, incorporating campfire pits, Brown Shingles are direct descendents of Muir's Hangnest.

Archival photos reveal a radically different landscape in the Bay Area a hundred years ago. Brown Shingles, originally built on barren grass-covered hillsides but now embedded in dense vegetation, suggested the forest in their materials and siting. The dense urban woods surrounding many Brown Shingles today is part of these places' original planning, an extension of their architectural motives. These houses were designed to eventually metamorphose into cabins in their own forests.

Travel to Yosemite in the 1860s was arduous and dangerous. Yet the place's pull was so powerful that a thousand tourists visited in the summer of 1869, the year Muir arrived, before even a stagecoach route was established. Famed landscape architect Frederick Law Olmsted, in his 1865 "Yosemite and the Mariposa Grove: A Preliminary Report," described the trek: "A man travelling from Stockton to the Yosemite… is commonly three or four days on the road at an expense of thirty to forty dollars, and arrives in the majority of cases quite overcome with the fatigue

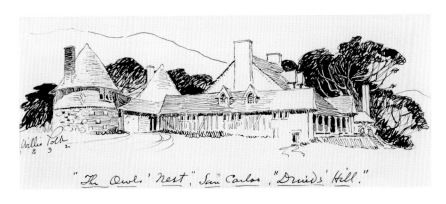

"The Owl's Nest," San Carlos, "Druids' Hill."

and unaccustomed hardships of the journey...many leave before they have recovered from their first exhaustion and return home jaded and ill." Those who braved the physical hardships faced other hazards as well. Black Bart, the gentleman stagecoach robber, plied his trade along the route in the 1870s.

Over the next forty-plus years, Muir and diverse companions made the trek many, many times, venturing well beyond Yosemite Valley deep into the wilderness. Incensed at the destruction of Yosemite by tourism, Muir became a powerful voice for conservation, founding the Sierra Club in 1892. In 1903, he took outdoorsman President Teddy Roosevelt camping for three days in Yosemite, convincing him to place Yosemite under federal control.

Intrepid and tremendously persuasive, Muir both promoted and protected the wilderness, exploring relentlessly, from Alaska to Africa, and repeatedly traveling to the West Coast's wild places. As Muir explained in *Nature Writings: The Story of My Boyhood and Youth*, he believed the wilderness resonates with a "natural wildness in our blood."

Enthusiasm for nature and the out-of-doors was certainly "in the blood" of those living in the Bay Area at the turn of the twentieth century. The drive to experience nature, as wild as possible, had a spiritual dimension—nature was seen by some as a conduit to God. Bay Area spiritual practices of all types extolled the divinity in nature. The emotional power of Yosemite and the redwoods, painted by William Keith and photographed by Eadweard Muybridge, was evidence of this.

Being outdoors was also thought salubrious, a way to maintain and restore physical and mental health. Robert Louis Stevenson sailed to California in 1888, the better to recover from tuberculosis, a disease afflicting many at the time. Sleeping porches connected to bedrooms, where residents slept out in often chilling summer fogs (then thought a healthy practice), were a standard feature of Bay Area houses until well into the 1920s. Though civilized and gracious, Brown Shingles retain more than a trace of Muir's "wildness." The Berkeley Hillside Club's 1906 pamphlet, laying out the tenets of hillside design, illustrated by Maybeck and probably written by the club's president, Charles Keeler, with Maybeck, famously declares, "Hillside Architecture is Landscape Gardening around a few rooms in case of rain."

The Artistic Life

A movement towards a simpler, a truer, a more vital art expression, is now taking place in California. It is a movement which involves painters and poets, composers and sculptors...we must live art before we can create it.
—CHARLES KEELER, *The Simple Home* (1904)

And "live art" they did! Brown Shingles provided settings for pageants and recitals, dances and readings, wholesome entertainments of all sorts (though Jack London's "stag room" at his never-completed, redwood-shingled Wolf House may have been intended for more raucous occasions). Berkeley was home to an abundance of writers and poets. Addison Schuster, an East Bay journalist writing in the 1890s, exclaimed, "There are more writers of verse in the East Bay than in any section of the United States."

Brown Shingles were designed for these entertainments—stair landings were often large enough for pianos, rods were rigged to create curtained performance areas as well as to separate spaces, and not infrequently full stages were part and parcel of the floor plans. Large sliding doors separated and opened rooms depending on the entertainment program. Maybeck was an enthusiastic pageant master, donning costumes even when not performing.

Bay Area artistic life was decidedly bohemian, often very eccentrically so. Though they might be professors

19

at the University of California or highly educated intellectuals, many Brown Shingle dwellers were fanatical about "natural" child rearing. The Maybecks were staunch adherents of this approach, which produced some dilemmas, as recounted in *Berkeley Bohemia*:

According to their daughter-in-law, Jacomena Maybeck, [the Maybecks] decided to cut loose from conventional structures and call their son "Boy" until he was old enough to choose his own name. Unfortunately, "Boy" chose a name that his parents hated. When he was about five, he decided to dub himself "Wollenburg" after Charles Wollenburg—a kindly neighbor who gave the child candy. His parents finally compromised by calling him "Wallen."

Berkeley's bohemians often lived in neighborhoods close to the university, with a particularly well-known cluster in an area known as "Nut Hill." In the heart of this neighborhood, on a site purchased from the Maybecks, is the Bay Area's most highly realized setting for the "Artistic Life." Though not a Brown Shingle, the Temple of the Wings, a pair of linked pavilions constructed of concrete Corinthian columns, was entirely open air. A radiantly heated floor and roll-down canvas walls, along with braziers for roasting nuts, kept the family warm. In 1909, the *San Francisco Call* in an article entitled "Back to Nature and the Greek" described the house's owner, Florence Boynton, as an "Alameda society woman, friend of Isadora Duncan, [who] sleeps

with her children on the roof, plays and studies with them among the flowers, banishes tight clothes and close rooms—all to arouse the souls of her babes."

Boynton, a teacher of modern dance, was also known for leading toga-clad figures through the adjacent woods. Her husband was a San Francisco businessman, apparently very good-natured.

Nature and art commingled in daily events throughout Bay Area summers and falls. From performances at Berkeley's 1903 Greek Theater to skits, readings, and performances arranged by the rich and famous at the men-only Bohemian Grove campground on the Russian River, fifty miles north, Bay Area residents eagerly supported and participated in small-scale and domestic artistic productions of nearly every type in houses that were built before the silver screen transformed the cultural landscape, putting such amateur entertainments deep in the shade.

Both Brown Shingle architects and their most persuasive proponents, Charles Keeler and Joseph Worcester, were familiar with and sympathetic to the political and artistic ideas of the English Arts and Crafts movement. In the hands of the architects Henry and Charles Greene, practicing primarily in Southern California, the Arts and Crafts ideal of houses built and furnished with handmade work of the highest level of craftsmanship received perhaps its most splendid expression.

Top A. C. Schweinfurth (for the office of A. Page Brown), Swedenborgian Church of New Jerusalem, San Francisco, California, 1894. This church embodied the beliefs and collaborative spirit animating the "Artistic Life" as well as the regard for nature at the root of Bay Area Brown Shingle culture. Courtesy the Swedenborgian Church, San Francisco

Center Jessie Matteson, Matteson House, Oakland, California, 1905. Lumberman and architect Jessie Matteson designed his remarkable Brown Shingle chalet as a meeting place for the Bay Area's Baha'i religion. The living room's picturesque and very unusual freestanding clinker-brick fireplace forms the center of a walk-around inglenook.

Above "Hawaiian House Showing Steep-Pitched Roof," from *The Simple Home* by Charles Keeler. Arguing against strictly functional roof forms, Keeler points out that steeply pitched roofs are not limited to places with heavy snowfall.

William Morris and John Ruskin's socialist ideas of inexpensive but highly crafted workingman's houses were more fully developed in California's bungalows than anywhere else. Brown Shingles, though they incorporate Arts and Crafts ideas, are a separate phenomenon. Richer, more complex, more experimental, occasionally capricious and playful, Brown Shingles are about life unfettered by social convention, promoting instead intellectual exploration, artistic sensibility, and fundamental connection to the natural world.

A Bewildering Array of Spiritual Practices
From mediums and mystics to Latter-Day Saints and Buddhists, the Bay Area at the turn of the century was home to an enormous range of spiritual practices. In 1894, the Swedenborgian Reverend Joseph Worcester built the remarkable Church of the New Jerusalem in San Francisco, with A. Page Brown as the official architect (though many accounts credit A. C. Schweinfurth in his office as the designer) and Maybeck as draftsman. Exposed madrone branches support the roof, paintings by William Keith line the walls, a window by Bruce Porter admits light above the altar, and an off-center fireplace at one end warms the interior, providing a cozy place for readings and furnishings designed by Maybeck. Though made of stucco to resemble a Spanish mission, the church exemplifies the values animating the Bay Area Brown Shingles—nature, art, and spirituality united, with the whole imagined as a domestic setting.

Brown Shingle houses resemble churches, while the churches of this period resemble houses. Consider the "cathedral ceiling"—structural framing, carefully assembled, is left exposed under a pitched roof, a common feature in Bay Area Brown Shingles. While Unitarian and Swedenborgian churches had a domestic scale, houses offered spaces for assembly, performances, and rituals.

Nontraditional spiritual practices—newly invented, ancient, and everything in between—flourished, with attendant "doctors" and health facilities. New and old practices coexisted, occasionally merging and morphing into one another. A fascination with exotic architecture had its counterpart in exotic religions. When Oakland's 1906 Brown Shingled Japanese-Swiss Matteson House became the meeting place for a group in the Baha'i faith, the owners' families disowned them. In the San Anselmo Brown Shingle known as the Igloo, featured in the following pages, Inuit totem poles flank the entry to the fire pit. The persuasive,

21

articulate, and charismatic Charles Keeler evolved from promoting *The Simple Home* in 1904 to become the creator of his own religion, the Cosmic Society, in the 1920s. This society met regularly in the backyards of its members. Candlelit services often included musical performances and sermons by Keeler concerning topics of interest to him, such as fairies. Even in the twenty-first century, cults and invented spiritual practices thrive in Northern California, occupying many repurposed older buildings alongside such venerable religions as the Society of Friends and Hinduism. Here witches remain ubiquitous, and traditional Western medicine often is regarded with deep suspicion.

Brown Shingle Architects

"If it's true that the eccentrics of the earth moved to America and the eccentrics of America to California, then the eccentrics of California have a special place in their hearts for [Berkeley]," quipped Wall Street Journal *reporter Ken Wells in an article on Berkeley at the end of the 1980s.*—It Came from Berkeley

Those who ventured to California at the turn of the century may not have been the most sane and conventional, and their numbers included many whose ideas might elsewhere have seemed radical. The architects then drawn to San Francisco, like their bohemian literary and artistic counterparts, were critical of the East Coast establishment's approach to their discipline. Young, optimistic, and ambitious, they hoped to build their own practices with adventurous, even bohemian clientele.

Among the first Brown Shingle architects, arriving in the 1880s, were Bernard Maybeck, whose completion of the program at the École des Beaux-Arts was followed by stints in architectural offices in New York and Kansas City; Ernest Coxhead, who left a London office to head to Los Angeles and work for the Episcopal Church, and who subsequently moved to San Francisco; and Willis Polk, who came to California, returned to New York, then reached California again, eventually bringing his father and brother. Maybeck, who lived in Berkeley, was the most thoroughly offbeat. In *On the Edge of the World: Four Architects in San Francisco at the Turn of the Century*, Richard Longstreth quotes Schweinfurth's description of Maybeck as a "freak," though this term was said to be intended affectionately.

The advent of the twentieth century brought a vigorous building boom and not coincidentally sustained a second influx of architects. Civic institutions initiated

Top The wood detailing in Matteson House is emphatic and enthusiastic, drawing from a variety of architectural sources. The redwood-paneled stair, typically a focal point in Bay Area Brown Shingles, is finished with triangular battens studded with large "nailhead" squares, a super-scale reference to a species of hand-made wooden vernacular joinery.

Above Arkin/Tilt Architects, Hester/McNally House, Berkeley, California, 1999. In the Bay Area, shingle construction is not limited to wood. This addition to a Berkeley residence, assembled from a variety of recycled materials, is clad in shingled metal license plates. Courtesy Ed Caldwell, Photographer

grand plans for San Francisco, including a master plan by Daniel Burnham (a close friend and relative by marriage of Joseph Worcester). Coxhead and Polk successfully lobbied for the selection of John Galen Howard to take charge of construction of the University of California beaux arts campus in Berkeley, the result of an international competition masterminded by Maybeck, in which Howard had placed fourth. (The competition's winner, Émile Bénard, elected not to supervise construction of his scheme.) Among many campus buildings, Howard also designed the redwood-shingled "Ark," in 1905, housing the university's architecture school, expanding it twice in the next few years to accommodate the demands of a thriving local profession.

A second generation of Bay Area Brown Shingle architects, many trained by the first, each built hundreds of buildings. Julia Morgan, a student of Maybeck's, was the first woman to attend the École des Beaux-Arts. Architect John Hudson Thomas graduated from Berkeley and, after a stint at John Galen Howard's office, opened his own firm. The largely self-taught A. W. Smith designed Brown Shingles throughout the Bay Area in a remarkable range of styles. Quirky shingle houses were designed by Maxwell Bugbee, a third-generation San Francisco architect, and even the more traditional Charles Sumner Kaiser—trained in the office of McKim, Mead & White (and who later changed his name to Charles K. Sumner at the outset of World War I)—was infected by enthusiasm for nature, designing houses with bark-covered tree trunks as columns and sleeping porches open to the sky. The Midwestern Greene brothers, Charles and Henry, trained at MIT and opened their office in Pasadena, designing their "ultimate bungalows," in which every last lamp and textile were part of the grand design. Enticed to Berkeley by the sister of one of their Southern California clients, they designed the Thorsen House, in Berkeley. Though the first group of architects was more radically idiosyncratic, the second designed many more Brown Shingles, with a great vigorous variety of architectural invention that has rarely been equaled.

Styles and Sources
In his short, influential 1904 manifesto, *The Simple Home*, Charles Keeler illustrated his arguments with just ten photographs. Among these were a Maori house in New Zealand, a Hawaiian thatched hut, and the Japanese Tea Garden in Golden Gate Park, the only building remaining today from the 1894 California Midwinter International Exposition. Exoticism was

the vogue. California designers felt an affinity with the wooden architecture of Japan, a country which had only relatively recently become known to the West, with Commodore Perry's visit in 1854.

The curves of Japanese and Asian roofs, tilting up at the ends; sliding doors and panels; layers and screens; elegant wood joinery detailing, employing Asian motifs; carefully designed, exposed wood structure—these elements are as integral to Bay Area Brown Shingle architecture as the tenets of the English Arts and Crafts movement. Then, as now, Bay Area architects cheerfully married William Morris's socialist ideals and his Arts and Crafts dictum, "Have nothing in your house that you do not know to be useful, or believe to be beautiful," with Asian wood-building traditions. Redwood proved an ideal material for interior woodwork, easy to shape, beautifully colored, available in burls as well as standard wood grains. Interestingly, even Shingle Style houses on the East Coast occasionally made use of redwood paneling imported from California!

Early Bay Area architects, in addition to their embrace of Asian forms, brought with them preferences for forms reminiscent of European, and more specifically English, medieval vernacular architecture. Maybeck developed a fascination with Swiss vernacular chalets when he revisited Europe to publicize the competition for the University of California campus at Berkeley, and soon enough the Brown Shingle vocabulary grew to incorporate an encyclopedic variety of architectural traditions. Julia Morgan's shingled 1905 North Star House in Grass Valley, for instance, marries an Italian Renaissance palazzo plan with very rustic materials drawn from the site—waste rock from the mine, log columns and shingles from the local trees. Simultaneously rustic and refined, primitive and sophisticated, such marriages of opposites epitomized the architectural culture of the Bay Area.

Earthquake, Fire, and Shingles
"Shingles, if left to themselves, rot very slowly and in a very clean manner. Since the grain of the wood is in the direction of drainage, the rot is constantly washed out instead of accumulating," advises Charles Keeler in *The Simple Home*. In this way, the simple redwood shingle surpasses the clapboard, or any other type of wood siding, and does not require paint. "Natural shingles last fully three times as long as a coat of paint, and are thus in the end an economy," continues Keeler. The existing Victorian buildings of the 1880s and '90s, painted and

embellished with decorative woodwork, were not only the wrong style, in Keeler's view, but also the wrong finish, and especially the wrong color.

Assembled in layers from the bottom of the wall up, shingles work exceptionally well to shed water and protect the structure beneath. Almost any flat, impervious material may be shingled—nineteenth-century miners flattened tin cans as siding, and twentieth-century Berkeley architects shingle license plates—though more traditional materials include clay, stone, and copper.

Redwood shingles, the basic units of Brown Shingle architecture, do far more than shed water. When allowed to weather naturally, they provide a primordial link to the forest, allowing residents to literally live in a redwood tree—in fact, often in a specific redwood tree, one logged from the site or saved for a unique purpose. The shingles' shapes and textures may vary—extra-long shingles or diamond-cut shingles or extra-thick shingles (shakes)—and their edges may have extra layers to provide a roll or upward curve, offering a variety of possible decorative effects.

The Brown Shingle's practical, symbolic, and expressive advantages do not constitute the entire story. The shingled cloak lends a specifically architectural magic. In and of itself, it has no particular correct or necessary geometry—unlike boards, brick, or stone. A shingled building may assume almost any shape while taking on the virtues of low cost, strong connections to nature, and potential for appealing textures and expression. Shingles easily accommodate unusual forms, difficult and expensive to make in other materials. In the late nineteenth and early twentieth centuries, shingles formed a stylistic glue, holding together a potentially chaotic collection of ideas and sources, the bass rhythm on which riffs were improvised. Absent a defining form itself, yet possessing great character and adaptability, the redwood shingle, in adept hands, offers tremendous possibilities.

The great coastal redwood trees survive, even thrive, in a region swept by frequent wildfires and racked by violent temblors. Clad in thick, fire-resistant bark, redwoods produce seeds requiring the enormous heat of a wildfire to germinate. Though terrifically tall, they are strong and flexible and rarely fall in earthquakes. Buildings constructed of redwood flex and sway, riding lightly the region's frequent shakes.

Milled redwood, though, is no match for fire, especially the superheated urban firestorms which have repeatedly swept through Berkeley and Oakland, generated by hot winds and an abundance of flammable vegetation. Great shingled retreats, deep in the woods, often burned before or soon after completion—Jack London's Wolf House by architect Albert Farr and William Randolph Hearst's Wyntoon, a masterpiece by Maybeck, are now nothing more than memories. The ruins of Wolf House, in a park named for London, are visited by thousands each year, while the Hearst retreat, secret and inaccessible, is known only by a few photos.

In the 1906 earthquake, San Francisco was devastated by fast-moving firestorms as well as by the army's demolition of wide swaths of buildings in a largely failed effort to stop the fire's advance. The loss extended to tens of thousands of wooden buildings. As a result, between 1906 and 1914, there was explosive growth in the number of Brown Shingle houses constructed in and around San Francisco. Shingles subsequently lost appeal as the Mission Style, realized in stucco, became much preferred by developers. The 1923 Berkeley fire destroyed hundreds of Brown Shingles, burning many houses by Maybeck, including his own. With this came the end of shingles as a popular building material. Even Maybeck abandoned them, experimenting instead with varieties of concrete walls and corrugated metal roofs. Charles Keeler's own Brown Shingle house, designed by Maybeck in 1905, miraculously survived the fire but was refinished in stucco at the architect's insistence.

The eccentric bohemian intellectuals of the turn of the century were the cultural ancestors of the Beat poets of the 1950s and the flower children and activists of the 1960s. When hippies picked up hammers, shingles reemerged as a popular building material, and the 1960s saw a minor Brown Shingle renaissance. Development of Sea Ranch, on the Northern California coast—guided by landscape architect Lawrence Halprin's plan to preserve the spectacular environment by limiting and consolidating building sites and with remarkable original buildings designed by Joseph Esherick and the firm of Moore Lyndon Turnbull Whitaker—led to a resurgence in the popularity of unpainted wood siding and wood shingles. The romance of Sea Ranch and the power of its highly original architecture inspired shingled and natural wood-sided buildings of all types throughout this country and others, and, with this, the shingle was reimagined as a modern material.

James Hubbell, Sea Ranch Chapel, Sea Ranch, California, 1984. Shingles afford, even encourage, expressive designs impossible with less elastic materials.

The occasional use of redwood shingles has continued, often in highly artistic houses. However, fire protection regulations on the heels of another devastating firestorm, in 1991, which incinerated thousands of houses in Oakland and Berkeley, in conjunction with the commercial depletion of old-growth redwood, have made redwood-shingle construction now both prohibitively expensive and, in some places, outlawed by building codes.

Fortunately, many Brown Shingles have survived the past hundred years, during which ideas of home design have been radically reinvented. Their owners contend with a variety of inconveniences: kitchens are too small, interiors are dark, bathrooms and closets are tiny. These are sacrifices happily made. Brown Shingles possess an emotional appeal with informal qualities that are generous and comforting rather than merely convenient. The cabin in the woods, the essential idea of the Brown Shingle, remains an enduring metaphor for dwelling in the Bay Area, as vigorous now as it was 125 years ago.

25

Brown Shingles

1891 to 1913

Top Laid out in the first decade of the twentieth century, the large neighborhood around Benvenue Avenue, seen here, in Berkeley consists almost entirely of Brown Shingle houses extending across into Oakland. Dwellings of similar size, on very similar lots, are designed with wide variations in architectural style and landscape treatment.

Above Along the Presidio Wall, several blocks of urban Brown Shingles line Pacific Avenue in Presidio Heights. Here, the best-known Bay Area architects of the late nineteenth and early twentieth centuries worked side by side and across the street from one another. On the famous 3200 block of Pacific Avenue are two houses by Ernest Coxhead (including the Waybur House) and Bernard Maybeck's Goslinsky House, adjacent to a house remodeled by Willis Polk.

Brown Shingles are a sociable bunch. They gather in neighborhoods, often varying dramatically in design though clad in the identical material. Enclaves of Brown Shingles still exist: many square blocks in South Berkeley, "Maybeck Country" in the Berkeley Hills, a few dozen blocks in the oldest part of Piedmont, a group of 1906 survivors at the summit of Russian Hill in San Francisco, several blocks of Pacific Avenue along the Presidio Wall in San Francisco, a group of professors' houses behind Stanford in Palo Alto, and small sections of most of the older Bay Area cities. Others are spread around the San Francisco Bay, surrounded by later neighbors, fitted to sites once remote. Still others are deep in the woods.

The most adept and creative architects, their most iconic Brown Shingle houses, and these places' archetypal natural settings are this book's foci. Houses by the earliest Brown Shingle architects—Ernest Coxhead, Willis Polk, and Bernard Maybeck—led to a group of houses by following generations of architects, including an interesting group of local practitioners who were primarily self-taught.

A hundred years on, Brown Shingles have much to tell us about the Bay Area's past. Built before everyone owned a car, before television, movies, and other distractions, when family life was more highly valued, these houses were designed to be intensively inhabited. Brown Shingles were the "party houses" of their day. Social entertainments and a complex family life, attended by servants, formed the daily program. Filled with window seats and inglenooks, public spaces in these houses were richly furnished, often finished in elegantly designed redwood paneling, focused on fireplaces built of rustic clinker bricks (the dark, misshapen bricks that were closest to the fire in the brick kiln). Seemingly casual outside, richly realized within, they were, as Charles Keeler said, "temples of family life"—welcoming, informal, yet with high purpose.

Architect Willis Polk freely combined modern ideas and medieval forms. At the portion of this double house built painter Dora Williams, a large, north-facing, Gothic-shaped window, located high up in the gable end, illuminates the living space, with a line of casement windows below.

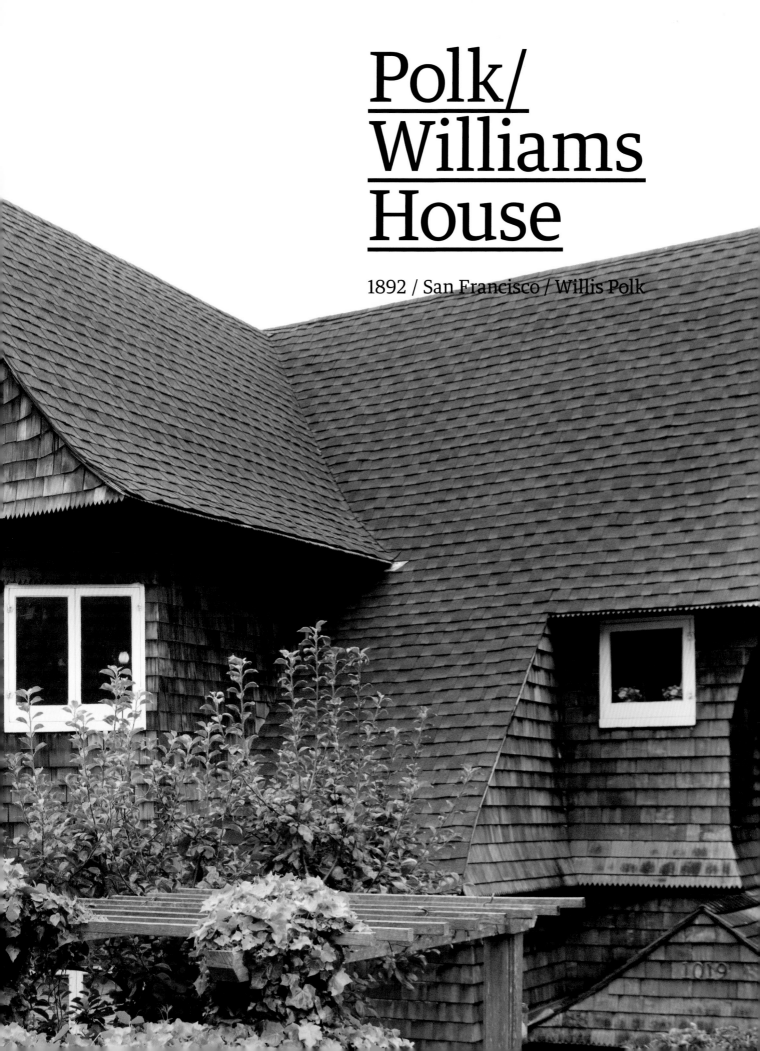

Polk/ Williams House

1892 / San Francisco / Willis Polk

Right Irregularly sized, unpainted shingles flare to form a kind of protective eave above the entrance to Polk's side of the double house.

Far right, top Two distinct gables, formally different but similarly sized and shaped, anchor each end of the street facade. The Polk residence is at the left, with a steep roof descending to two small eyelike windows, while the Williams residence gable to the right admits north light to the painter's studio.

Far right, bottom The Williams residence's porch is supported by elegantly proportioned Doric redwood columns. An eccentrically placed long, low window lights the stair inside.

Willis Polk was a very small man, barely five feet tall, with a large personality, "the *enfant terrible* of San Francisco architecture, the brash, outspoken critic, the stuntsman, the *bon vivant*, always broke," according to William Kostura in *Russian Hill*. In 1891, Russian Hill was not a stylish place; the newer, "better" Victorian houses were being built in Pacific Heights and the Mission District. Reverend Joseph Worcester lived at the Hill's summit, adjacent to a set of shingled cottages he had designed in 1888. For his own residence, Polk renovated an existing house belonging to prominent Russian Hill developer Horatio Livermore, located across the street from Worcester. When Polk's father and brother moved to town to join him in business, he purchased a double lot next door, in concert with painter Dora Williams, designing a single building to house the two families. Mrs. Williams's lot was forty feet wide and relatively flat; Polk's was twenty feet wide, precipitous, and presumably far less expensive. Dora Williams was the widow of well-known painter Virgil Williams, founder of the San Francisco Art Institute. Her close friend, Fanny Stevenson, came to live in the house for a time after the death of her husband, Robert Louis Stevenson. Over time, the summit of Russian Hill became a Brown Shingle enclave, as well as a center of bohemian culture and social life.

The Polk and Williams shingled houses are medieval in appearance, though with modern bands of windows as well as a large, arched, north-facing window dominating Mrs. Williams's living room. Polk paired rustic, cabinlike redwood-paneled rooms with elegant classical redwood details. Miniature Greek temples form part of the railing on the Williams side and also adorn a tall clock in the studio atop the Polk House. Both sides are dominated by stairs which perambulate up, down, all around, linking spaces in these very vertical houses in dramatic sequences. In Polk's house, the more vertical of the two, the stair climbs from the entry to the top, passing a middle floor reached by a third stair from the generous landing. Tiny servants' stairs were concealed in closets.

Designed with mind-boggling spatial sophistication, these small houses do not feel cramped, and they served as settings for frequent gatherings. Scaled-down elements, especially railings little taller than two feet, as well as window seats and other built-ins, contribute to a shiplike feeling of snug comfort.

Facing Vallejo Street, the house is picturesquely massed, with a gable for each family. On its east facade, though, the Polk residence spills down the hill, ramshackle-looking and apparently all improvisation. Rumor has Polk deliberately designing this elevation to look like "the back," thumbing his nose at the residents of the adjacent and elite Nob Hill, who were daily faced with this disorderly view of Polk's house.

Opposite The Polk residence's gallery, at the top floor, looks down into a tour de force of multilevel stair design. Complex-looking, the stair is far smaller than it appears—the top-level railing is just over two feet tall! The Greek Temple–fronted grandfather clock, original to the space, matches the railing design in the living room of the Williams residence.

Left, top The stair landing in the Polk residence, lined by a row of casement windows, is less a pause than an intersection. In one direction, a flight of stairs leads up to the gallery level (opposite), while in the other direction, a smaller stair leads up to the mid-level sitting room (left, bottom).

Left, bottom This intermediate-level sitting room is both part of the generous gallery/library above and an intimate setting adjacent to the brick fireplace.

Opposite, top Remarkably, the Brown Shingle enclave atop Russian Hill survived not only the 1906 earthquake and subsequent fire, but also the U.S. Army's demolition of the surrounding area in an effort to halt the flames. Courtesy Carol Ann Rogers and the California Historical Society

Opposite, bottom At six stories, the Polk residence is organized around a series of sitting rooms connected by the mind-bogglingly complex stair. Just inside the street door, prefiguring the stairs beyond, visitors climb a few steps, to a long window seat forming one end of the living room.

Right, top Polk was a careful, eclectic student of his own architectural details, with a library of sketchbooks holding source materials. This diminutive classical volute in the Williams residence, carved in redwood and used to support a very simple mantel, is modeled on very grand sources.

Right, bottom An Ionic redwood column marks the beginning of the stair; and adjacent, attenuated Doric column balusters frame the view to an arcade of recessed wooden arches above the large brick fireplace.

Carrigan House

1892 / San Anselmo / Ernest Coxhead

Englishman architect Ernest Coxhead's domestic work often alludes to his native country's medieval buildings, including those constructed, all or in part, of thatch. The elegantly proportioned Carrigan House has few actual straight lines. Dormers emerging from the great roof curve along their edges to form swelling, Gothic-arched architectural elements.

Right, top The long, sweeping roof, lined with dormers, rises up at both ends. These subtle adjustments, among many others, convey the impression that the house has settled into its site some, perhaps over its apparently long history. An unidentified photographer made this image when the house was just completed. Courtesy Mary Ann Beach and Richard Longstreth

Right, bottom The house dissolves into its now mature landscape, with a porch, now enclosed, to the south, and a sequence of trellised terraces at the opposite end.

Far right, top Both the five-sided bay and porch on the south end were originally designed to appear as though additions to a seemingly much older building.

Far right, bottom The generous ground-floor porch, now glazed in, is unusual in Bay Area Brown Shingles, where the summer climate is far cooler than in the East Coast.

Some houses survive the insults of history only through the force of their architectural presence. The Carrigan House has had a colorful, difficult life: abandoned for years with reports of cows in the living room and pigeons roosting upstairs, used as a speakeasy during Prohibition, and then reclaimed for family life in the mid-twentieth century.

Even its earliest days were marked by unhappiness and transition. The house was built for the Carrigan brothers, Andrew and Louis, by their father, who owned a wholesale hardware company in San Francisco. When Andrew's marriage to his new wife quickly failed, ownership of the house passed to Louis and his own young wife, Madge. Not long after, Louis died, and the house became the property of his widow, a dedicated traveler.

At first glance, the house appears to be architecturally traditional, perhaps a Georgian-style country manor rendered in brown shingles. On closer inspection, though, it becomes clear that Coxhead experimented and combined a much wider variety of architectural ideas. The house's roof is one long gable with a ridge that sweeps up at its ends, perhaps suggesting a sagging centuries-old thatched roof, or perhaps reflecting an Asian influence. Along the long front facade, a stucco bay with a very large stepped window, supported on one end by a buttress, interrupts the stucco-and-shingle wall. A large porch, its roof supported on Doric columns, projects from the south end (now enclosed). The Carrigan House appears far older than its years, as though it has been repeatedly remodeled by successive generations.

Within, the house possesses an open plan, though on several levels, with large rooms partially separated by screens, reminiscent of East Coast Shingle Style country houses. The roof's long ridge is matched by a gallery-style hallway ending in a broad stair to a room-size landing in the projecting bay; the large stepped window visible on the facade corresponds to the interior stair.

With views to Mount Tamalpais along the entire length of its rear facade, the Carrigan House once overlooked extensive grounds. While its 1892 design reflects an imagined history, the intervening 120 years have provided events just as intriguing.

40   **Right** A terra-cotta medallion,
suggesting an ancient family
history, is glimpsed through the
ivy by the front door.

Opposite Coxhead's mastery of the
redwood shingle includes not only
a wide variety of shingled wall patterns, textures, and geometric ornament, but also extends to highly
picturesque manipulation of the size
and shape of shingles themselves.

Opposite Terminating a long, wide gallery along the entry facade, and a half level up, this luminous landing forms a setting for musical entertainment. At the facade, the large window is stepped to reflect the stairs inside, a signature Coxhead device.

Right Redwood can be rough and rustic or turned, carved, detailed, and elegantly finished. This lively, idiosyncratic stair railing's balusters are turned with alternating narrow and thick spirals.

Above A large bay window is accented by window seats, and a decorative partial-height redwood screen wall frames the living and dining areas as parts of a larger space.

Opposite Coxhead possessed a wry architectural sense of humor. Secret doors, detailed as part of a wood-paneled wall, were standard features in his houses. Here, a concealed door leads to a room behind the living-room fireplace.

Churchill House

1892 / Napa / Ernest Coxhead

Prosperous Napa banker Edward Churchill hired Ernest Coxhead to design this
house, adjacent to his own, as a wedding present for his son. A redwood tree on
site provided the lumber. The new house—a picturesque assemblage, with a steep,
rounded roof sporting a pair of slightly ominous-looking dormers, a round tower
resting on very short Doric columns, and a large, nine-part window with a baroque
arch at its center, the whole finished in unpainted shingles—could hardly be less
similar to the father's elegant, shingled Victorian. The generation separating the
two dwellings had wrought radical change, from the prim outlook of the Victorian
age to the beginnings of the influence of the Bay Area's bohemian culture.

In *On the Edge of the World: Four Architects in San Francisco at the Turn of the
Century*, Richard Longstreth notes that Coxhead freely arranged a variety of elements from diverse architectural origins, employed at different scales, without feeling the need to resolve them. At its exterior, the Churchill House appears complex;
and the round entry tower suggests a house of several stories. The building, in fact,
is substantially less grand.

The younger Churchill's house became a local landmark, known as much for memorable parties and performances as for its striking design. A wide, elaborate stair,
leading to a commodious landing which incorporates a bay over the entry porch,
was arranged around the staging of plays and musical performances.

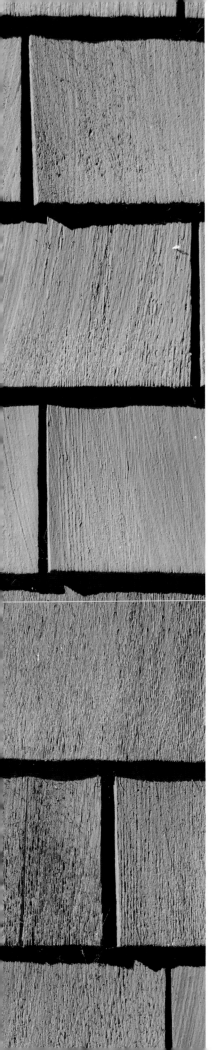

51

Rolled around the corners, the Churchill shingles are fashioned not only to curve around, but also to bend down, demonstrating the redwood shingle's remarkable plasticity, here to an effect reminiscent of the round corners of medieval thatch.

53

Far left A generously wide stair leads to an ample mezzanine, and beyond that to the second floor. In its earliest years, the Churchill House was known for its entertainments—these mezzanine spaces were carefully arranged for staging performances.

Above With its elegantly detailed redwood paneling and coved plaster ceiling, the living room is raised several steps from the entry yet well below the mezzanine.

Left Near the fireplace, at the window, an eclectic Spanish Colonial arch—a nearly unprecedented rendering of Mission Revival forms in redwood—is set into a large, multipaned, otherwise English Palladian window. Another signature Coxhead device, a window similar to this can be seen in his own house in San Mateo.

Siegriest House

1900 / Oakland / A. W. Smith

A particularly prolific architect, A. W. Smith was a master of the picturesque. With the Siegriest House, pointed metal gables and tower tips, exaggerating, distorting, and rendering vivid the place's simple masses, caused this house to become a local landmark from its earliest days.

Right and far right, top The house was designed to be approached at a picturesque angle, so that both the upraised gable ends and the metal roof tips are seen to maximum effect. The corner bay's steeply conical pointed roof is the source of the place's popular name: the Witch's House.

Far right, center This old postcard shows the original water tower and the early landscape, far different from the lush garden engulfing the house today. Courtesy Barbara Loomis and Stephen Elspath

Far right, bottom Now completely overhung with ivy, the shingled water tower building evolved into a painting studio for the owner's son. Louis Siegriest was the youngest member of the Bay Area's Society of Six, a group of local painters in the 1920s known for especially colorful, unkempt landscapes.

The ebullient A. W. Smith was among the most prolific Bay Area architect of his time, with hundreds of buildings to his credit. In the article "The Shingled House in California," Smith describes the practical as well as the artistic advantages of building with shingles: "Not having to paint his house, the owner of a shingled residence trains his vines and climbing roses over the walls, secure in the thought that every two years he does not have to take them down and hire a gang of white-overalled daubers to put on a thin film of lead poison." Smith was largely self-taught, though he worked for a time in the San Francisco office of architects Bliss and Faville. Because Smith designed in a breathtaking variety of styles over thirty-five years, his buildings are not easily identified, though many share some characteristic details.

The Siegriest House in Oakland, with its round, pointed turret, has long been a neighborhood landmark. Do the upturned gable ends reflect the influence of the Japanese Tea House, built in the 1894 San Francisco Midwinter Exposition as a permanent gift to Golden Gate Park? Or is the source actually the East Coast Shingle Style, which often incorporated short, round towers and wraparound porches? Smith was an architectural omnivore, absorbing then recombining many influences.

Like their architect, Louis and Amelia Siegriest were colorful figures. Though he began his career driving horsecars, Siegriest made a fortune as a developer. His son, Lou Siegriest, who continued to live in the house after his parents were gone, was a well-known painter, the youngest member of Oakland's Society of Six. This group of iconoclastic painters, outsiders in their own time, were known for their vividly colorful paintings with a focus on landscape and light. Lou converted the house's water tower into his painting studio and applied his painting palette to some of the less public parts of the house. Now largely surrounded by smaller, far less original houses and lush, mature landscaping, the Siegriest House, with its distinctive, broad-brimmed, pointed conical turret, is known by some as the "Witch's House."

59

Opposite As with most Bay Area Brown Shingles, a generous light-filled stair is a prominent feature. Opening to the porch beyond, the entry is through a dense, mature garden rather than onto the nearby street.

This page This detail of the unusual newel post at the base of the stairs is an example of hand-carved, classicizing, simultaneously Ionic and floral ornament.

Opposite At the upper level of the round turret, a semicircular window seat, set beneath a line of large windows glazed with curved glass, opens to the master bedroom.

61

Above Built-in window seats, a signature device of Bay Area Brown Shingles, are employed throughout this house. In the dining room, a corner bay expands the room, with window seats designed to allow this relatively small house to accommodate large groups of people.

Left Yet another window seat, this time at a stair landing, makes this space a destination as well as a passage.

Waybur
House

1901 / San Francisco / Ernest Coxhead

Along the edge of the San Francisco Presidio, the 3200 block of Pacific Avenue is built with a remarkable set of urban town houses clad in Brown Shingles and designed by many of the best-known Bay Area architects of the late nineteenth and early twentieth centuries. Here, a pair of Coxhead houses, the Waybur House, center, and a house for the painter Bruce Porter, face across the street to houses by Bernard Maybeck and Willis Polk.

Brown Shingles fit naturally into Berkeley's lush gardens, surrounded by redwoods planted by their owners and by picturesque landscaping and walks. Yet Brown Shingles were also built in the city, creating "that distinctive San Francisco ambiance resulting from the union of urban form and rustic materials," as John Beach noted in *Bay Area Houses*. Nowhere is there a more impressive collection of these rustic urban dwellings than on Pacific Avenue, particularly the 3200 block, adjacent to the Presidio Wall. Brown Shingled town houses line both sides of the block, with a pair of dwellings designed by Coxhead facing a Maybeck-designed house next door to a Willis Polk renovation. Julia Morgan, Albert Farr, the Newsom Brothers, and a crowd of other Brown Shingle architects also contributed to this unique urban streetscape.

The Waybur House, recently placed on the National Register of Historic Places, is at once the most elegant and the most iconic of these. Flanked on both sides by Brown Shingles (including another Coxhead-designed house built at nearly the same time for Julian Waybur's brother-in-law, artist and writer Bruce Porter), the building seems at first glance a classical Georgian town house, symmetrically disposed around a large Palladian window.

65

There is, though, very much more at work. The wide front door is framed by a shallow-arched Mannerist pediment, looking like something borrowed from Michelangelo's Laurentian Library in Florence. Above this is a Palladian window, featuring the requisite Serlian motif. Across this, a stepped, architecturally uncanny railing follows the line of the stairs at the building's interior. Robust decorative architectural elements are all rendered in black-painted wood and set into a very plain field of unpainted redwood shingles. By contrast, the rear of this house (and all the others along this side of the street) is composed as an irregular facade, appearing as if no architect had been involved in its design.

At the interior, a large, intricately realized stair—a redwood structure all its own within the larger structure of the building and filled with light from the eccentric Palladian window—ascends three stories, from the dining area at the first floor, to the living room and music room, where Waybur offered music lessons, on up to the bedrooms at the top. Large sliding doors permitted the music room to be private, or, on special occasions, opened wide to the rest of the house.

Pacific Avenue's blocks of contiguous Brown Shingles adhere to an elegant model of urban design like that found in the great cities of Europe. Here, though, even the most urbane setting is not far from nature: the wild natural landscape of the adjacent Presidio is these houses' backyard.

Left At the street facade, classical detail, at once elaborate, sophisticated, and painted black, is set into a very plain, rustic shingled wall.

Above Taking cues from a Georgian town house, the Waybur House is symmetrical around a large Palladian window. Yet Coxhead wrenches this symmetry at the facade's center, above the shallow arch over the entry, with a very unusual balcony, rising from right to left, which follows the lines of the interior staircase.

69

Opposite, top The kitchen, at the back of the house, looks onto the green of the Presidio. With its white marble counters and white-painted wood cabinets, it employs the palette and materials of kitchens of the early twentieth century.

Opposite, bottom At the redwood-paneled living room, the large plate-glass, double-hung windows, advanced for their time, are original elements.

Above Paired archways, at right angles to each other, lead to the living room (to the left) and a smaller music room where Julian Waybur gave piano lessons.

Unlike many of his contemporaries, the ebullient Bernard Maybeck was devoted to the range of polychromatic architectural effects. Here, finished elements, built of smooth-surfaced redwood, are painted in oranges, reds, yellows, and a turquoise blue, contrasting with the background field of rough, unpainted redwood shingles.

Flagg House

1901 / Berkeley / Bernard Maybeck

Equal parts practical architect and romantic visionary, Bernard Maybeck campaigned for years to build a great beaux arts "City of Learning" on the University of California campus. He proposed an international competition, with the world's most accomplished architects submitting their schemes. Eventually, he convinced the university's board of regents, as well as his patron Phoebe Hearst, who financed Maybeck's visit to Europe promoting the competition. It was on this trip that he came under the spell of an especially simple type of domestic vernacular, the Swiss chalet, which would, like so many other building forms, contribute to his design work. (Maybeck's European tour promoting the campus competition proved a huge success, bearing out Maybeck's vision—with 105 initial entrants, the eventual result was construction of one of the finest, most extensive beaux arts campuses in the country.)

The house of classics professor Isaac Flagg, completed in 1901 and the first of three Maybeck built for the academic on an acre in North Berkeley, marks the beginning of Maybeck's work with the Swiss chalet form. With its widely overhanging eaves supported on cigar-shaped struts, overscaled, painted wooden cutout balustrades, and colorfully painted trim, this chalet is a remarkable reinterpretation of the Tyrolean model in which structure and ornament were integral, with carved beams, struts, and cladding evolved into a highly expressive, coherent assemblage of elements. At the interior, the architect included an inglenook adjacent to his first outsize Jacobean-style fireplace, the first of many which would become a Maybeck trademark. During his European tour, Maybeck had met the great English architect Richard Norman Shaw, and this house's inglenook may have been inspired by Shaw's picturesque designs.

The house's rooms are organized around a complex, commodious stair, whose width and three-story height make the house feel far grander than it in fact is. The wide, inviting stair leads to a large room on the third floor, open the length of the house, with a generous sleeping porch to the east and prow-shaped window seat on the west. Designated on plans as a room for entertainment, this turn-of-the-century "great room" enjoys spectacular views of San Francisco Bay through unusually large west-facing windows.

Professor Flagg, realizing that he needed an escape from his family in order to concentrate on his work, asked Maybeck to build a separate library on the property. Later, another house for his son was ordered up. Much later, Maybeck's friend and biographer, Ken Cardwell, lived for many years in the house built for the professor's son.

Left, top A built-in seat adjacent to the large Jacobean fireplace creates a cozy inglenook, an intimate space within the larger living room.

Left, bottom Rising to three stories, this extra-wide, light-filled stair makes an inviting trip to the room at the top floor—a space open the length of the dwelling and home to the place's well-known entertainments.

Opposite The gilded burlap wall covering, stone fireplace surround, and a Maybeck-designed chandelier are original to the dining room.

Long and narrow, the Gregory House is richly articulated along its western facade, where covered outdoor spaces reach into the exterior wall and alternate with interior living spaces. Here, John Galen Howard, architect of the nearby beaux arts University of California campus, responded to a familiar Berkeley Hills quandary—the contest between orienting the house west toward magnificent views of San Francisco Bay and protecting the house from the ferocious afternoon western sun, its blinding effects amplified by reflections off the water.

Gregory House

1904 / Berkeley / John Galen Howard

Left, top Along its back, the Gregory House meets the hillside covered with oaks and natural vegetation. At the second-story, east-facing sleeping porches—a long-lived Bay Area tradition—allow residents to awaken to morning's light in a very natural setting, almost as if they were camping out.

Below, left With dormer windows and covered outdoor spaces facing San Francisco Bay, the house is long and thin, much of it one room wide.

Below, right Both house and garden provide for life out-of-doors, and it is the smallest leap to imagine Sadie Gregory holding class here.

Webs of friendship and acquaintance permeate the Brown Shingle story. Sadie Gregory, whose grandson Daniel Gregory has written this volume's preface, figures in several of these. A woman of keen intellect who studied with Thorstein Veblen and taught at Wellesley College, she and husband Warren Gregory were close friends with architect John Galen Howard, beginning when Howard (with his family) moved to Berkeley in 1902 to supervise the construction of the University of California campus.

In 1904, the Gregorys hired Howard to design a summer house in North Berkeley (on Nut Hill), which they enlarged after the 1906 earthquake to become their full-time residence. In 1912, the Gregorys provided Howard a corner of their property to build his own house, and Sadie educated both sets of children in a school she established in that house. The Gregorys hired Bernard Maybeck, who lived around the corner, to design other Gregory family summer homes nearby, and they hosted an architectural salon of sorts at their home, attended by students and professors from Berkeley's architecture school, housed in the Brown Shingled "Ark," another Howard design. Later, Sadie befriended William Wurster, helping launch his career in 1929 with the commission for a farmhouse in the Santa Cruz mountains. Eventually, the Gregorys sold their Berkeley home to Wurster, who headed Berkeley's architecture department and who later developed famed Greenwood Common on a flat portion of the grounds west of the original house.

The Gregory House is organized off of a wide, gallery-like hall, along which porches alternate with living space. The deeply recessed entry canopy was built around a great tree, with an opening in the roof to accommodate the trunk. That opening remains today though the tree has long since disappeared. An overscaled brick fireplace at one end of the great hall dominates the living room, where architectural salons were held. Upstairs, bedrooms lead to sleeping porches along the house's eastern facade.

Even more than most Brown Shingles, this house incorporates its site into the plan, establishing more the feeling of a summer camp than a year-round residence. Both the Gregorys and Howards loved to camp out and live outdoors. This house, very close to the open-air Temple of the Wings, gives form to the idea that Brown Shingle living was just a more civilized type of camping.

Opposite Originally, entry to the house
was through a covered space surrounding
a great tree. Today, only a skylight remains
to mark the location where the tree
reached up through the roof.

Below, left Paneled throughout in a simple, elegant redwood board and batten, the carefully detailed ground floor is archetypal of early-twentieth-century Bay Region Style interiors.

Below, right At the dining area, the house is one room wide, with doors opening to the exterior at both the east and west sides. A large brick fireplace allows the house to be kept warm in chilly weather, though in very close proximity to the out-of-doors.

Bottom A wide, glazed gallery, linking the living and dining rooms, steps gracefully up the slope. Modern light fixtures were installed throughout the house by William Wurster, dean of Berkeley's architecture department and among the most important and prolific Second Bay Region Style architects, who lived here in the 1960s.

Below Wide, covered sleeping porches open to bedrooms, encouraging residents to roll their beds outside during warmer months.

Kofoid House

1905 / Berkeley / Julia Morgan

"Small but mighty" would describe architect Julia Morgan, five feet tall with a body of work encompassing more than seven hundred buildings. Morgan was extremely modest, eschewing publicity for her highly regarded work. Her modesty, however, did not prevent her applying year after year to the prestigious École des Beaux-Arts in Paris. When finally admitted, she was their first woman student. Born in Oakland, Morgan studied engineering at Berkeley under her lifelong mentor, friend, and collaborator, Bernard Maybeck. He encouraged her journey to Paris and application to the École, his alma mater. Julia graduated, leaving Paris in 1902, just before the arrival of another influential American woman from Oakland, Gertrude Stein. And modesty did not prevent her going toe to toe with her client William Randolph Hearst, one of the most self-possessed men in American history, as they together built, and occasionally rebuilt, his supremely eclectic California castle, San Simeon.

Her buildings are well constructed and carefully detailed, rendered in an extraordinary range of styles, and, though focused on the clients' particular needs, her houses possess broad appeal. Like many of Morgan's clients, Charles Kofoid—marine biologist, Berkeley professor, and a founder of the Scripps Institute in La Jolla—and his activist-suffragette wife, Carrie, were highly intelligent, politically active, and well-traveled.

For the Kofoids, Morgan designed a gambrel-roofed Brown Shingle, and, soon after, she designed an adjacent dwelling for Professor Kofoid's father. The heart of the Kofoid House is the professor's library, a redwood-paneled retreat lined with bookcases, with a fireplace and situated alongside a trellis-covered porch. The Kofoids assembled a collection of more than forty thousand scientific books, which eventually outgrew the library and filled the father's house next door.

The entry, facing a side yard, follows a pattern often employed in Berkeley Brown Shingles, frequently constructed on long, narrow lots. Side entrances led to central entries and stair halls, leaving both ends of the house available for banks of rooms free of circulation while simultaneously providing generous routes to rear gardens.

87

Top Above Dr. Kofoid's study, the former sleeping porch has been enclosed and forms another study.

Above Politically active and a suffragette, Carrie Kofoid came from an adventurous family. Here, she sits in the living room surrounded by animal pelts brought home by her widely traveled missionary sister. Courtesy Frances Mitchener

Above A zoologist, Dr. Kofoid collected forty thousand books, which soon overflowed the walls of his study and living room, shown here, and eventually filled his father's house, also designed by Morgan, built next door.

Left Extra-deep windowsills in the dining room make the room feel especially commodious while also modulating the effects of glare where dark interior paneled spaces meet the bright outdoors.

Above In the living room, wide, generously scaled redwood moldings join wall and ceiling.

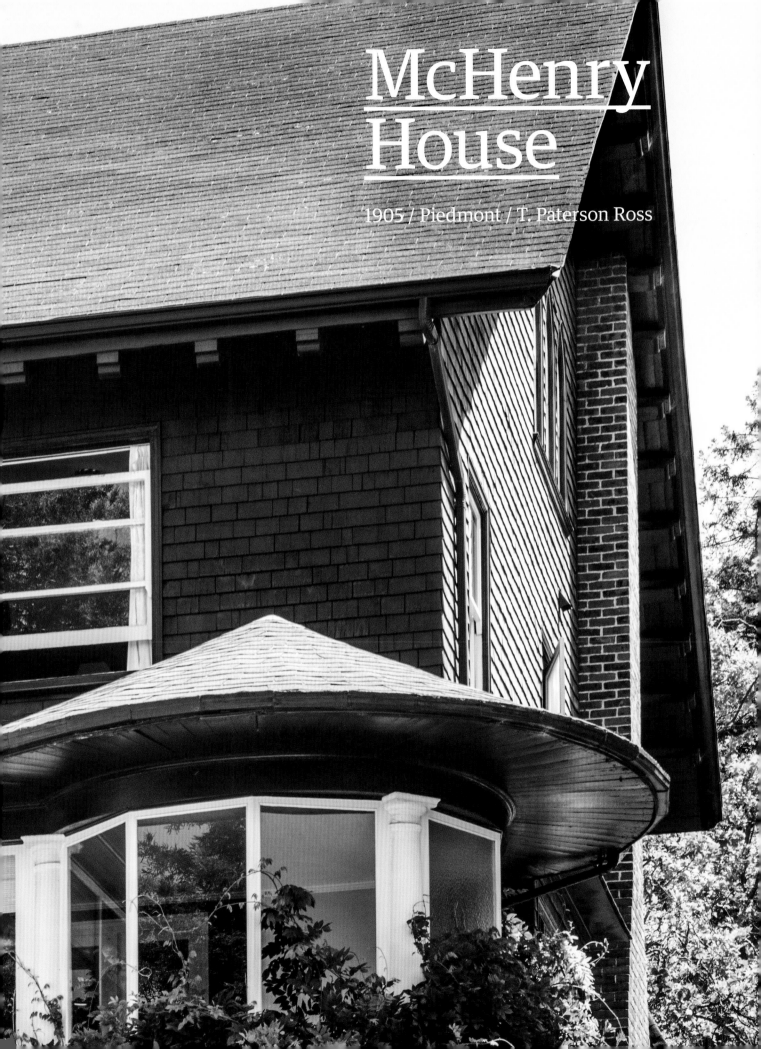

McHenry House

1905 / Piedmont / T. Paterson Ross

Residents of the small, conservative, well-to-do East Bay town of Piedmont might
be surprised to learn that their town's earliest and most distinctive buildings have
bohemian roots. Though Piedmont is known as home to famed politicians and
tycoons, including Secretary of Defense Robert McNamara, and financial figures
Dean Witter and Charles Schwab, it is also the setting for the iconic 1877 brown
shingled cottage designed and built by influential Swedenborgian minister Joseph
Worcester—the first Bay Area Brown Shingle.

Through Worcester's Swedenborgian ministry and William Keith's paintings depict-
ing the Piedmont cottage, the dwelling came to represent the ideal of incorporating
nature into daily domestic life, and in time a substantial neighborhood of Brown
Shingles grew up around the cottage. The 1905 McHenry House, with its remarkable
projecting framework constructed of heavy redwood timbers, is among the most
memorable of these. Unique, with no well-known architectural precedent, its overscaled fretwork is a virtuoso performance of carpentry. Brown Shingles often chal-
lenge their builders, with round towers and flared walls and roofs, as well as rolled
and bunched shingles. These technically difficult, handcrafted, highly picturesque
elements are central to their terrific appeal—effects impossible to achieve in less
plastic materials.

The McHenry House, with its window seats, redwood-columned entry hall and
stair, and leaded glass windows at the stair and front door, is a high-style Brown
Shingle of this period. Just before and for several years following the 1906 San
Francisco earthquake, Brown Shingles designed by unrecorded architects and
builders (and usually not nearly so handsome as the McHenry House) were constructed in middle-class and well-to-do neighborhoods throughout the Bay Area.
For these few years, architects and their clients, employing a wide range of eclectic
sources, developed a remarkable collection of regionally distinctive, intellectually
and emotionally resonant, handsome, and highly realized dwellings.

T. Paterson Ross, architect of the McHenry House, was a Scot who arrived in San
Francisco at the age of twelve. In partnership with engineer A. W. Burgen, Ross had
a prolific post-earthquake career, producing a host of civic and commercial buildings in a wide variety of styles that contribute much to the architectural character
of San Francisco. Perhaps best-loved are his Moorish/Byzantine Islam Temple of the
San Francisco Shriners, now the landmarked Alcazar Theater, and Chinatown's Sing
Chong and Sing Fat buildings.

The McHenry House features
a very unusual projecting
wood-latticed facade.

Opposite A bay window, with original stained glass in a floral motif, illuminates the generous, winding stair and hall.

Above A flanking pair of Ionic redwood columns, set on half walls, form the entry to the living room from the foyer.

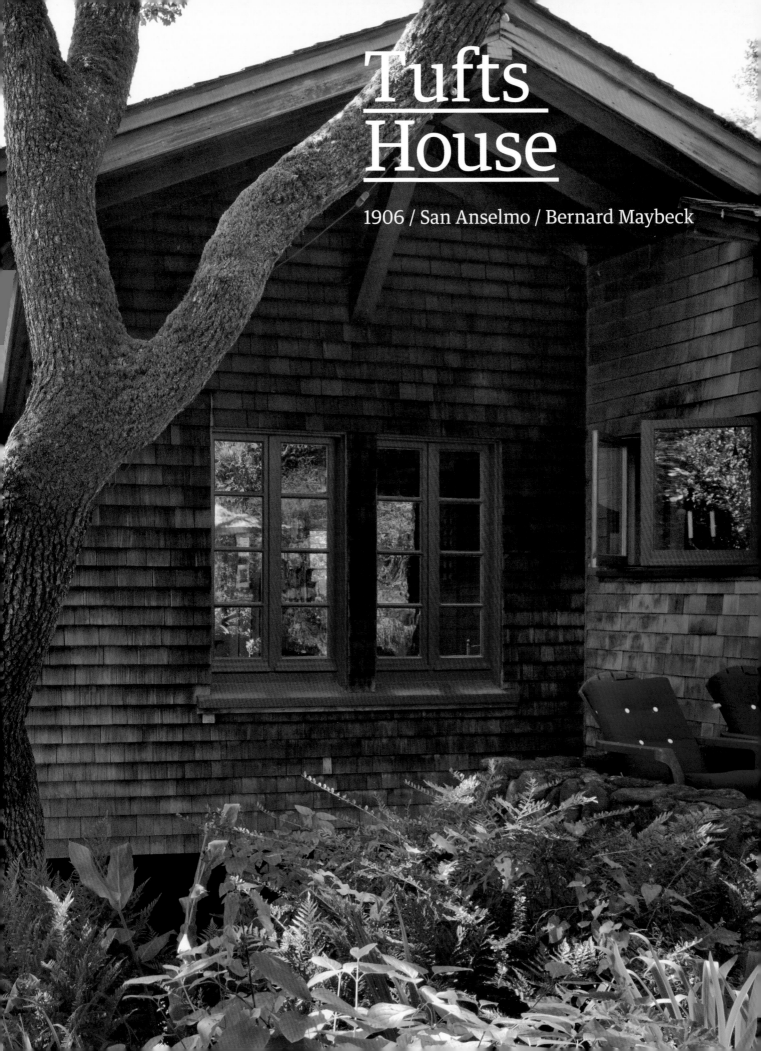

Tufts House

1906 / San Anselmo / Bernard Maybeck

Previous pages The first of three dwellings designed by Bernard Maybeck for the artistic Tufts family seems part cabin in the woods, part light-filled aerie.

Far left With its battered walls, projecting top bay, and tall retaining wall below, the house has an exaggerated height and the place appears a tower from the approach.

Left, top Now surrounded by mature oaks, this hilltop Brown Shingle, with its remarkable lacy trelliswork, must have appeared a very different place when it was just completed, a little more than a hundred years ago.

Left, bottom At its back, the house becomes a one-story cabin, merging into its site with its decks, terraces, and verdant landscape.

103

Though best known for his singular, eccentric, highly creative buildings, Bernard Maybeck possessed another talent at least as important as his artistic skill: he was very charming. Building a project with Maybeck was fun, especially for artists like the Tufts. They took such pleasure in this house that they built two more houses with Maybeck, the last next door to Maybeck's son's home, in the heart of Berkeley's Nut Hill.

This place in San Anselmo, called Tufts #1 in the annals of Maybeck lore, was built atop a hill in one of the warmer corners of the Bay Area. Though surrounded today by mature oaks (planted by Maybeck), the architect originally created a connection to the landscape with layers of hovering trellises composed of a delicate pattern of redwood sticks.

The house's simple, squared-off, brown-shingled exterior, with its lacy trellises, does not prepare the visitor for its interior. A path leads through the trees to a recessed front door opening into a dim redwood-paneled entry hall, a wide stair to the side. As the stair rises and turns, it widens further into an open, light-filled volume with views out in all directions. Passing a Maybeckian newel post-*cum*-Gothic light fixture, visitors turn to face an overscaled fireplace with three tracery-filled rondels. With French doors to a porch on the view side and to a patio on the other side, the living room runs the length of the house and is surprisingly formal. In concert with the huge fireplace, heavy pairs of carved redwood brackets provide a medieval air, in keeping with the Gothic tracery. As with other Maybeck houses, the overscaled elements make the house seem larger than it in fact is and offer a tangible sense of mystery.

Near the entry, tall, narrow, vividly colored windows are simply detailed and appear cut into the rustic, unfinished redwood-shingled wall.

Opposite The redwood-paneled staircase, only dimly lit at its lower level, climbs dramatically into a bright, sunlit, book-lined landing on the main level.

Top The long living room, designed for gatherings and entertainments, is spatially articulated by two pairs of heavy redwood rafters that descend the walls as brackets. While both end bays are light-filled and lead to outdoor terraces, the darker center bay frames the formidably proportioned fireplace.

Above Golden Gothic fretwork, set into three large redwood panels, ornaments a mantel extending to the ceiling above the overscaled living-room fireplace.

Right Maybeck-designed light fixtures, formed as golden Gothic, carved-redwood quatrefoil fretwork, illuminate the central stair.

Van Sant
House

1906 / Berkeley / Ernest Coxhead

Previous pages Reached via a winding path across a creek and through a very large Japanese-style garden, Coxhead's last Brown Shingle house occupies an idyllic, sylvan setting.

Far left, top View of the modernist, Second Bay Region-Style Stromberg House from the garden of the Van Sant House.

Far left, bottom Ideally sited to overlook Claremont Creek, the house appears set in a wide, expansive garden. In fact, it is part of a suburban neighborhood surrounded by other houses of various dates and styles.

Left, top In 1965, the house's idyllic setting was made to accommodate the nearby modernist Stromberg House. Decades later, the pair share their remarkable landscape in harmony.

Left, below A wide Dutch door leads into the house, and the porch beyond affords a perfect, layered view of the creek, terraces, and garden in the distance.

111

This is the last of Coxhead's Brown Shingles. The place shares a garden with three other architecturally notable houses, including a contemporary Coxhead house finished in stucco to its west and a modernist Brown Shingle to the east. A wide arch at the center of the house's shingled wall opens to a deep porch and a Dutch door leading to the entry hall. Originally, the porch ran the width of the front, forming an outdoor room beneath an ancient oak. Inside, the house is carefully arranged for entertaining. In the living room, a landing raised only a few steps up, and large enough for the piano, provides a stage for the room, which is otherwise focused on its clinker-brick fireplace. The complex stair is characteristic of Coxhead, featuring a very low railing and concealed doors built into the paneling at the corners of its landings.

Anthony Bruce, the current owner and an architectural historian and director of the Berkeley Architectural Heritage Association, has maintained the house much as it was when he grew up in it. Anthony recalls the 1965 construction of the adjacent modernist shingled house, more or less in his former front yard, as a terrible event in his childhood, deeply disturbing to his parents.

Almost fifty years on, the fences have come down, and the two Brown Shingles, young and old, enjoy a complementary relationship with the creek-side garden, each building highlighting the other's adept, elegant siting. Like their houses, the current generation of owners have become friends. And though very different architecturally, both houses are refined examples of their respective times, and of that Brown Shingle imperative of living in touch with nature.

Original shingles have been retained where possible and highlight the difference between then and now, as well as the impressive longevity of original old-growth redwood.

Top, left In the years before movie theaters, radio, and television, Brown Shingles were frequently employed to stage homegrown entertainments. This large landing, just off the living room, was an excellent stage for musicians and performers.

Top, center Demonstrated by this view into the study from the living room, rooms could be opened to each other, while large sliding doors or curtains afforded the flexibility to separate spaces.

Top, right In addition to the open plan, very large living room windows overlooking the garden underline the place's relative modernity. In other respects, this house, like many designed by Coxhead, could be imagined as an older building updated over time.

Bottom, left This pair of photographs of the living room, taken forty years apart, shows the stair hall with the dining room beyond. The current owner, who has lived here for more than forty years, is at once the dwelling's resident and curator.

Bottom, right The living room interior as it was during the era of the Van Sant family. Courtesy Ruth Van Sant Dodge and Bettina Van Sant Deyl

115

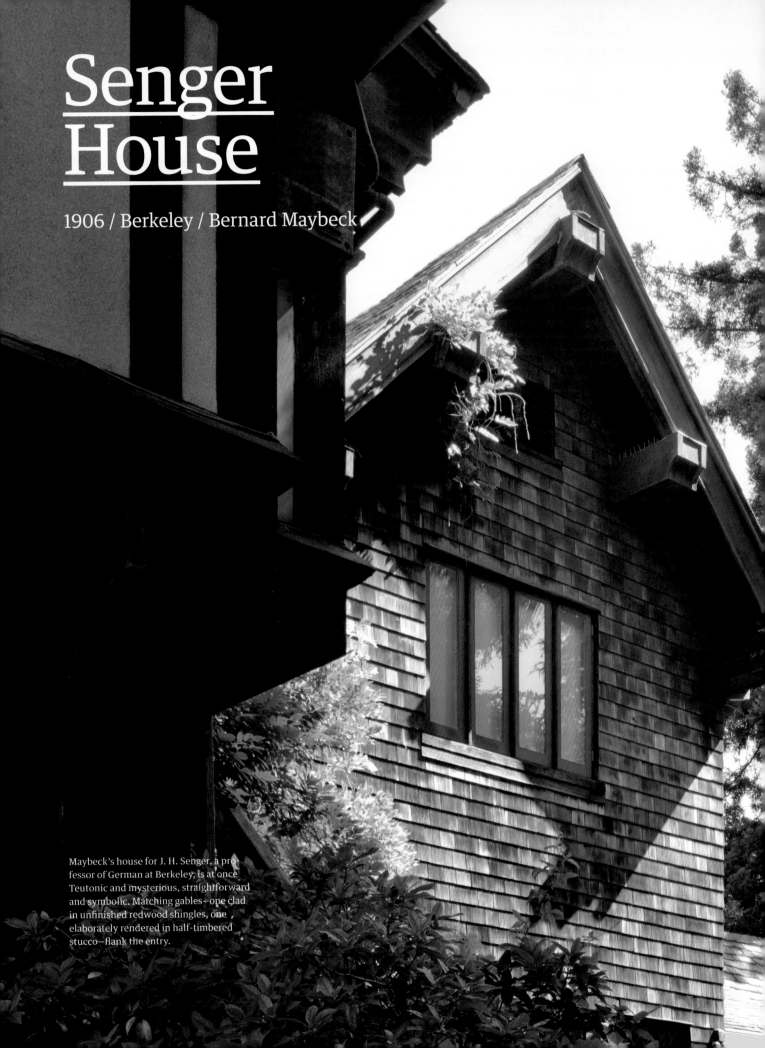

Senger House

1906 / Berkeley / Bernard Maybeck

Maybeck's house for J. H. Senger, a professor of German at Berkeley, is at once
Teutonic and mysterious, straightforward
and symbolic. Matching gables—one clad
in unfinished redwood shingles, one
elaborately rendered in half-timbered
stucco—flank the entry.

Ring in the love of truth and right [...]
Ring in the thousand years of peace
—"In Memoriam"

These lines, by Alfred, Lord Tennyson, are inscribed into the Senger House's baronially scaled fireplace and set the mood for this remarkable dwelling. Medieval Teutonic imagery is stenciled throughout the house and carved into overscaled architectural woodwork—a Maybeckian evocation of his client, a professor of German at the nearby University of California. Set closely alongside its North Berkeley street, the Senger House, like other Brown Shingles, follows an unusual logic in siting—a source of these places' great variety. Rather than occupying the center of their sites, these houses often hug their property lines, leaving wide swaths for large, sunny gardens. Stretched adjacent to the street, the Senger House transforms along its length from a simple Brown Shingle exterior to a half-timbered stucco building ornamented with stencils. As it rounds the corner, the far more ornate stucco facade morphs into an elaborate Maybeckian arrangement of extended, broken eaves and decorative crossed beams inset with carved ornamental devices.

The everyday front door appears in the long facade centered between two tall narrow gables, identical except that one is shingle and the other stucco. At the west facade, a more formal entry leads to the music room, physically set off from other spaces at the house's interior and employed for more ceremonial occasions. What can we make of this transforming facade, whose west end literally mirrors its east, though made in different materials? In *Bernard Maybeck* (1992), Sally Woodbridge points out the shingled side holds the more casual, service-oriented functions of the house, while the stucco end is more formal, civilized. While this is true, must there not also be a more poetic intent? Perhaps these differences represent a marriage of opposites, or the evolution of an old-world German aesthetic toward a more rustic Californian one.

Inside, an overscaled redwood stair with Maybeck's characteristic cutout wooden balustrade rises through a story-and-a-half space. The L-shaped living space leads to a porch and to the generous, south-facing garden. Records of the original house and remnants of curtain hardware along the beams reveal that pairs of fabric panels partially separated the major interior spaces. Maybeck, the most evocative and atmospheric of architects, was equally at home designing sets for pageants and plays as he was working out dwellings, and the lines between the two are often gloriously indistinct. This place, with its music space and floor levels congenial to performances, is at once home and theater.

Left At the dwelling's formal street frontage, the half-timbering is made to emerge from the stucco, becoming fully three-dimensional. The house's west facade is an extravagant, Maybeckian fantasy, with broken pediments, heraldic devices, and stacked and layered ornamental brackets.

Center View of the railing at the rear of the house; scroll-cut redwood boards, in decorative profiles, here perhaps inspired by Germanic folk art, were a favorite Maybeckian technique.

Right The quatrefoil pattern on the iron gate at the west facade is another characteristic Maybeck motif.

123

Opposite, upper left and right The intricately planned, ornamented, and finished stair possesses a near-Baroque complexity and reaches to five levels. As with many other elements here, it suggests a ritual or ceremonial past. Carved, cut out, stenciled, mysteriously illuminated, and somewhat baffling, the stair is, in a way, a theatrical prop intended for everyday use.

Opposite, lower left Constructed entirely of redwood, the breakfast nook includes a pass-through to the butler's pantry.

Opposite, lower right The breakfast nook is set off from the dining area by a few steps. Originally, the separation was more emphatic, with drapes installed here and at several locations on the main floor. At the stair, the newel post bears a large, carved, medieval-style S, for the original owner's name.

Above A flamboyant baroque stucco fireplace mantel is stenciled with a quote from Alfred, Lord Tennyson's "In Memoriam."

James House

1908 / Berkeley / Charles Sumner Kaiser

126

Long sections of redwood tree trunks, their rough bark still attached, have been occasionally employed as overscaled, rustic columns in Brown Shingle architecture. Simultaneously reminiscent of the forest, the primitive hut, and other signal rustic structures, the rough log column possesses an iconic power. In other parts of the country, unpeeled logs may be found in forest camps and buildings off the beaten track, but in Berkeley, they are downtown.

The James House, designed for Berkeley High School principal Morris James, marries a rough, rustic exterior with a finely turned-out redwood interior. The front facade, visible through trees along a picturesque walk up from the street, features a gable with upsweeping eaves, making the house seem a Hansel and Gretel cottage, though this place precedes the whimsical "Storybook" period in Bay Area architecture by more than a decade. A redwood-paneled hall leads from the double story-height entry hall to a very fine Brown Shingle living room, with arched redwood brackets at the ceiling, French doors to the porch along the room's side, and a massive clinker-brick fireplace.

In 1906, after a visit to Berkeley, architect Charles Sumner Kaiser left his home in New York, where he worked for the large, polished, highly successful firm of McKim, Mead & White. Like others before him, Kaiser, once arrived in California, went native, designing a group of highly picturesque Brown Shingles for adventurous clients. With the advent of the First World War, he redesigned his name, becoming Charles Sumner before moving to Palo Alto, where his highly eclectic design approach led to work in a wide variety of architectural vocabularies.

Among Brown Shingles' appealing features are the rich textures and patinas of aged redwood. These shingles, now more than a century old, have acquired strikingly different color and texture due to their varying exposures to sun, wind, and rain.

129

Opposite A tall, top-lit stair hall, whose redwood-paneled stair rail is detailed like the adjacent walls, forms an entry at once spacious and complex, providing a generous scale to this otherwise modest house.

Above, left The living room fireplace is designed as a tall brick wall, at whose midpoint a series of corbelled courses step forward to form a mantel.

Above, right A large bay window in the small wood-paneled library gathers soft light ideal for reading.

Left Highly finished, substantial redwood beams, brackets, and joists at the living room ceiling—this house's structural system—provide a large part of its architectural character.

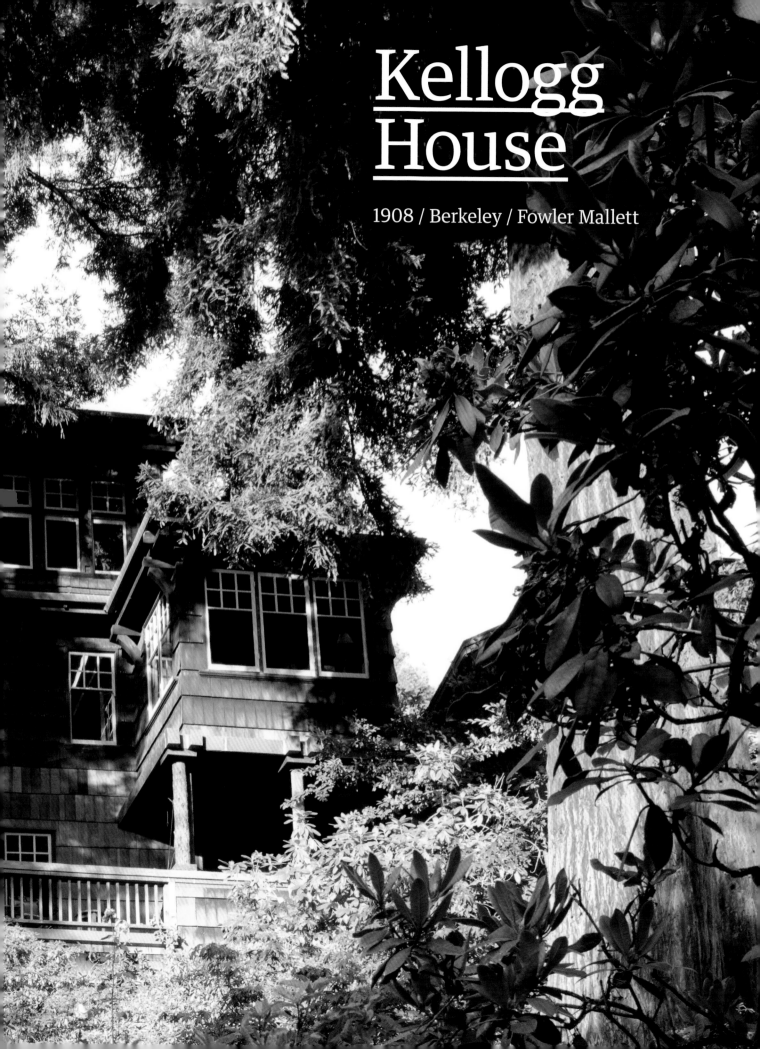

Kellogg
House

1908 / Berkeley / Fowler Mallett

Previous pages Redwood trees shade the rear of this house by the little-known Bay Region architect Fowler Mallett. Redwood tree trunks, their bark still attached, support covered porches at every level.

Right An elegant line of curved redwood brackets supports a trellis across this house's front, which today is concealed by dense wisteria vines.

Far right Bark-on-redwood tree trunks, typical at the decks and porches on this house, raise up a trellis at the upper-level balcony.

Right, below A clinker-brick pedestrian bridge leads from the street to the entry. Once common, few of these bridges remain.

134

Brown Shingles are characterized by their principal material, redwood, employed as boards and framing, woodwork and ornament, and, of course, shingles. Redwood burls and bark-covered logs; shaped redwood beams and waxed paneling; redwood brackets, carved classical and rustic decoration; redwood cutout and turned railings; redwood slabs, trusses, windows, doors, posts, cabinets, built-ins, and casings are the fundamental language of Brown Shingles. A second set of materials and elements are typical as well. Chief among these are clinker bricks, often employed with fireplaces and as landscape and foundation walls. Named for their distinctive sound when dropped, clinker bricks are the outermost bricks in the kiln during firing and so receive more heat, becoming purplish and deformed—the ideal material for rustic Brown Shingles. Other hand-worked materials include forged metals, primarily wrought iron, copper, and steel, worked into light fixtures, railings and fences, and hardware. In addition to their metal fittings, houses of the period were often furnished with hammered metal lamps, desk sets, vases and a variety of decorative objects, often made up in copper.

The Kellogg House in Berkeley, designed by little-known architect Fowler Mallett for a medical doctor, incorporates all these materials, often in striking ways. Clinker bricks, here assembled in a tall, arched structure, form a pedestrian bridge from the street. Not uncommon in their day, few clinker-brick bridges have survived the ensuing temblors and onrush of automobiles. Dining room paneling is fashioned from graphically patterned redwood burl, and large, shaped redwood brackets support the living room's arched ceiling. Redwood logs support trellises over the sleeping porches. The steel and copper fireplace facing was produced by Dirk van Erp, the renowned Dutch-American metal artisan, who opened his Art Copper Shop in Oakland in 1908.

Little is known of the architect, though he is said to have possessed an especially bohemian demeanor. Certainly Mallett's talent extended to making places where Berkeley bohemians feel right at home.

Extra-long shingles, often favored by late-
nineteenth- and early-twentieth-century
Bay Region architects, clad the exterior of
this highly crafted dwelling.

Opposite This shingled wall rests on
clinker-brick foundations adjacent to the
redwood grove at the rear yard. These
trees were planted shortly after construction was completed.

Far left The very tall living room, its
ceiling resembling medieval English
half-timbering and supported on curved
redwood brackets and chords, has excellent acoustics. Its owner, a pianist, has
installed a pair of pianos.

Left The unusual steel and copper fire-
place hood was built by well-known Bay
Area Arts and Crafts metalworker Dirk van
Erp in 1908, the year he opened his Art
Copper Shop in Oakland.

Tibbetts House

1909 / Berkeley / John Hudson Thomas

The most eclectic of the very eclectic group of late-nineteenth- and early-twentieth-century Bay Region architects, John Hudson Thomas drew from design sources that were both wide-ranging and, when assembled in a building, unexpected and provocative. This house, for the daughter of a land baron from the heart of Northern California's giant redwood country, is by turns chalet, castle, and, from certain angles, monastic retreat.

It is said that the Tibbetts House was built from a single redwood tree. In 1866, Canadian Duncan MacKerricher established his Laguna Ranch in the middle of the Redwood Coast, a stretch in Northern California then home to an estimated 1.4 million acres of old-growth redwood. In the midst of a region dominated by the logging industry, the Laguna Ranch raised sheep. The story goes that MacKerricher cut a great tree at his ranch, one perhaps thousands of years old, had it milled, then warehoused the lumber to build a house for his daughter, Edith, when she married.

Edith married Frederick Tibbetts, an engineering professor at Berkeley, and the couple hired architect John Hudson Thomas to design their home in North Berkeley, asking that he employ the legendary lumber. The dwelling is a virtuoso performance in redwood cladding, with a multistory tower built of horizontal redwood boards, a middle level of brown shingles, and an upper level in wide vertical boards with battens. At the interior, highly figured redwood burls form much of the paneling and door casings. The house seems suspended in the trees, with window seats and an overscaled trellis at the entry extending into the woods. A fireside inglenook, entirely fashioned from a single burl, forms a separate seating area at the living room's heart, with a music nook tucked behind. Whimsical copper light fixtures, designed by Thomas, resemble long-horned sheep and appear throughout the main floor. (Thomas became a close friend of the family, reportedly living there several years later while he constructed a house next door.)

Though the great, ancient tree provided a home built for the ages, the marriage quickly failed; the professor left Edith for his secretary. Edith, it seems, enjoyed her newfound freedom, leading a busy social life as a "club woman" and traveling widely. At the end of her long life, one entire bedroom was filled, floor to ceiling, with her spectacular collection of fancy hats, which now resides in a hat museum in Texas.

143

144

Above Now largely concealed by the forest, a trellis-covered walkway leads to the entry.

Opposite The house's extreme verticality is heightened by the approach from the street, which leads up a carefully choreographed sequence of stairs.

Above A commodious inglenook forms an edge of the living room and is said to be built entirely of wood from a single enormous redwood burl.

Right The architect, a family friend of the client, may have been alluding to Mrs. Tibbetts's father's sheep ranch with the whimsical design of these light fixtures.

Opposite Though apparently deep in the woods, wide bay windows with built-in seating, like this one in the dining room, gather sufficient daylight to prevent the place's being at all gloomy.

More than any other Brown Shingle in Northern California, the Greene brothers' Thorsen House was conceived as a complete work of art. From the careful yet elaborately developed clinker-brick walls, paths, and stairs that fit the house so beautifully to its site, to every wood, metal, and glass detail, no element of this dwelling escaped its architects' attentions.

Thorsen
House

1909 / Berkeley / Greene and Greene

The last of Charles and Henry Greene's "ultimate bungalows," though located in Berkeley, owes equally to Northern and Southern California traditions with shingle architecture, as well as to Japanese woodcraft. This dwelling is very far from "simple": the Thorsen House is a lavish eighteen-room spread designed in all aspects as a work of architectural art, including its remarkably realized furniture (now belonging to the Gamble House in Pasadena). With its low-pitched, widely overhanging roofs and complement of exotic materials, including many species of hardwoods, the Thorsen House has perhaps more in common with the Gamble and Blacker Houses in Pasadena than with other Bay Area Brown Shingles.

Mrs. Thorsen was, in fact, Mrs. Blacker's sister, and she hired the Southern California-based Greene brothers because she wanted a house similar to her sister's. Daughter of one lumberman and wife of another, she had the means to indulge her wish. And yet the house is at home in Berkeley. For all its subtle, carefully worked-out finery and rich, not quite maniacal detailing, this dwelling is meant to *appear* rustic and sophisticated, like its Bay Area counterparts.

The Thorsen House, like other houses by the Greene brothers, transforms simple wood construction into a fine art. From elegantly detailed, highly expressed wood-and-metal joints to the eased corners and Japanese-inspired shaping of its exposed wood members, wood elements were selected for the inherent beauty of their grain, precisely installed in certain positions, and lovingly finished so they appear as furniture. Lighting, bookcases, and cabinets are built-in, parts of a congruent architectural whole.

Japanese-inspired motifs, reflecting the Greene brothers' admiration for the craft of wooden Japanese buildings, together with nautical devices, reflecting William Thorsen's love of yachting, appear throughout the house. The master bedroom, originally affording an unobstructed view to San Francisco Bay, projects from the front of the house in a prow shape, providing a place for Thorsen to work while overlooking the boats he loved. Situated at the end of Greek Row, above the Berkeley campus, the Thorsen House connects gracefully to its site with clinker bricks, wrought iron gates and walls, and careful landscaping. Through sheer serendipity, the Thorsen House became the home of the Sigma Phi fraternity in 1943. The fraternity brothers hold "work parties" every Saturday, tending to the house and landscape.

A screen wall and bridge between two parts of the house, this tour de force of wood joinery and craftsmanship, assembled in the Japanese manner without nails, exemplifies the expressive possibilities of redwood.

Left, top With many of their houses, the Greene brothers developed signature decorative devices, replayed in various ways, scales, and materials throughout a dwelling. Here, the stepped "cloud lift" motif is visible in the mullions at the bay window illuminating the dining room. This Japanese-inspired detail is found throughout the house in a range of elements.

Left, bottom At the living room, recessed ceiling lights, glazed with stained glass, are set in a decorative wooden framework. At the top of the wall, a panel stenciled with floral motifs makes the transition from the wood-paneled walls to the ceiling.

Opposite The nickel-steel living room fireplace surround, inlaid with delicate bronze tracery, is set in a glazed tile wall inset with equally intricate mosaic tile designs.

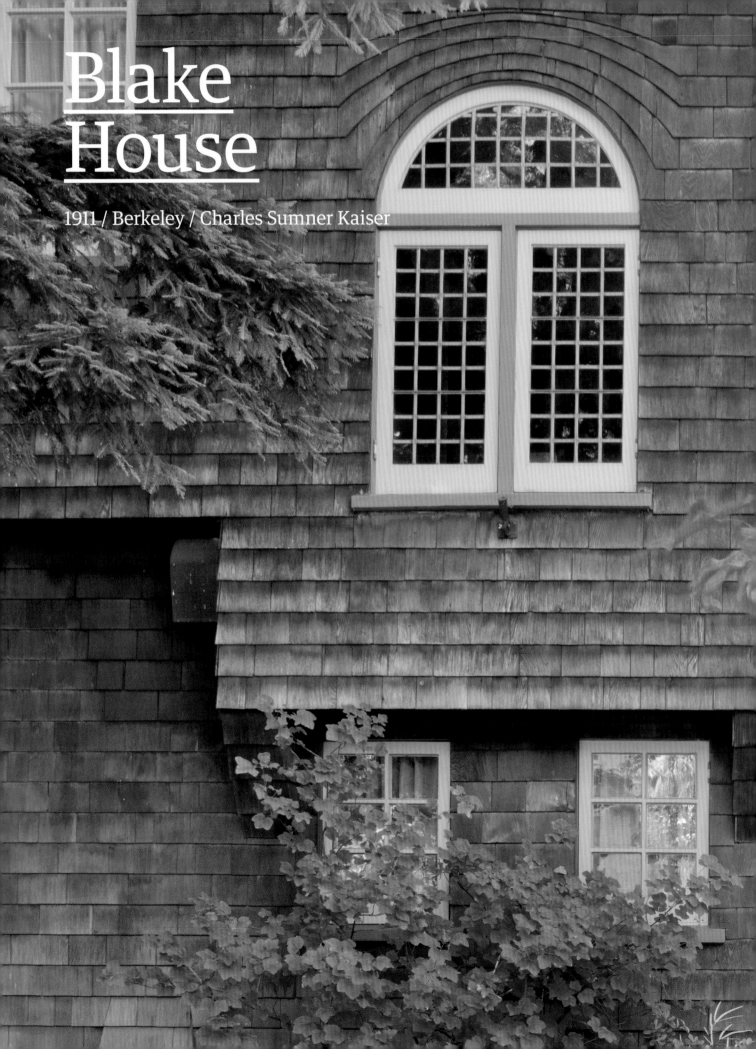

Blake House

1911 / Berkeley / Charles Sumner Kaiser

Previous pages Charles Sumner Kaiser assembled "quaint" architectural elements—upturned eaves, arched openings with bunched shingles over their tops, combinations of small and larger windows—with a modern sensibility.

Right The long roof here sweeps down from three stories to cover the entry, providing an intimate scale to this not small dwelling.

The English Arts and Crafts movement, with its roots in John Ruskin's socialist ideals of a house for every workingman and William Morris's beliefs that houses and their furnishings ought to be beautifully designed, handmade, and elegantly utilitarian, was familiar to Brown Shingle architects and to many of their clients. Filtered and reinterpreted with Berkeley resident Charles Keeler's *The Simple Home* (1904), this approach suggested settings for living the Artistic Life, and being connected to Nature.

Charles Kaiser's Blake House, more than many of his other Brown Shingles, is inspired by one of the architect's favorite sources, English cottage architecture, and takes more from English Arts and Crafts than most Brown Shingles. The current owners have fitted the house with period furnishings and installed wallpaper faithfully reproducing some of the period's most popular designs. Yet unlike English Arts and Crafts houses, this dwelling is clad in redwood shingles. Believing fresh air to be healthy, hardy Brown Shinglers slept out throughout the summer and fall months, although many Bay Area nights were windy and fogbound. (Even today, Bay Area houses are routinely built without air-conditioning and arranged to promote natural cross-ventilation. Visitors from less temperate climes find Bay Area homes too cold in winter, while Bay Area natives fling open their windows and switch off the heating wherever they travel.) Consequently, Kaiser designed the Blake House with sleeping porches (here, unusually, without a roof) for his health-conscious clients.

Left The earliest shingles could be extra wide because first-growth trees were not only larger but stronger than the trees that replaced them.

Opposite Above the arched windows, the dimension of the shingle overlap is narrowed, as though the field of shingles were a pliable skin, stretched back to reveal the opening.

Opposite A commodious wooden bench, deep, shady entry porch, and a wide front door form an especially hospitable entry.

Left, top Beyond the front door, past a set of interior curtains, a wood-paneled hall leads to a tucked-away stair, its reach up and out of sight.

Left, bottom Sliding glass doors open the dining to the living room. Period furnishings encourage an especially accurate sense of Brown Shingle interiors a hundred years ago.

163

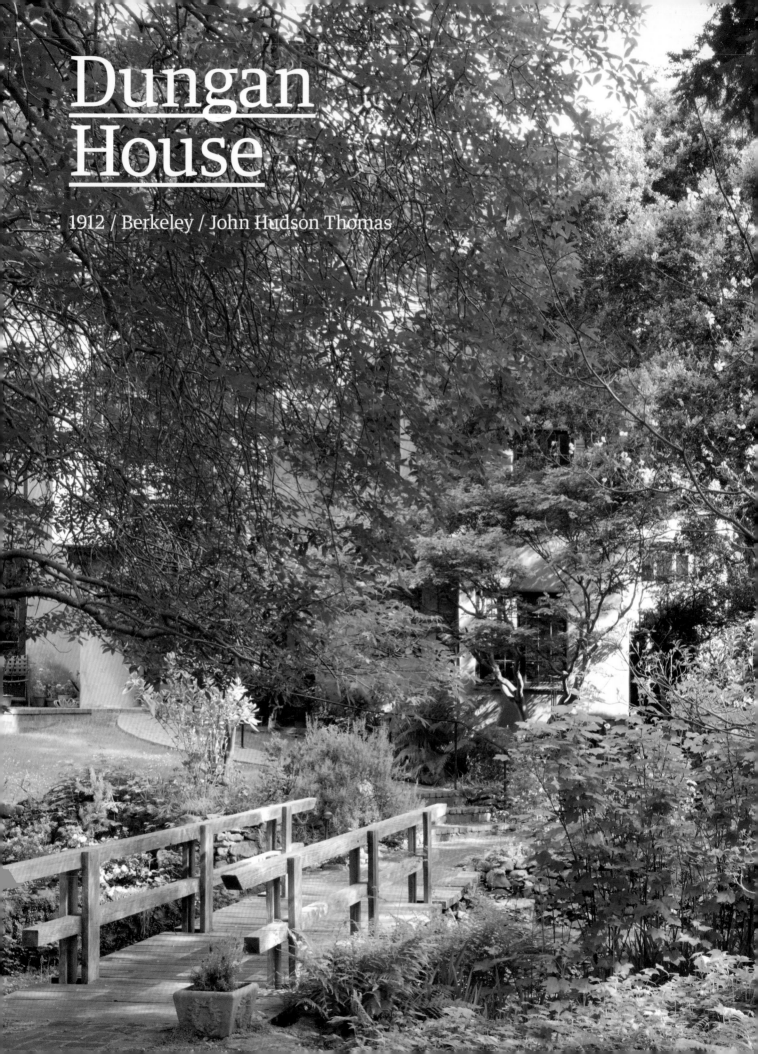

Dungan House

1912 / Berkeley / John Hudson Thomas

Wildly eclectic—here Bay Area cabin, there ancient British, half-timbered manse— sited to span Claremont Creek, with its forms stretched out vertically, like taffy, this discordant masterwork takes tidy Arts and Crafts domesticity in the most unexpected directions.

Far left, top A long, wide redwood balcony, projected from the living room, spans across the slow-moving creek below.

Left, top Tall gables, both overhung in wisteria, intersect a lower gable above the entry.

Far left, bottom Originally, exposed redwood framing was juxtaposed with redwood shingles. Later, portions of the board siding were faced with stucco as the house's cladding, enhancing the sense that the place was built over time. From *The Architect and the Engineer*, May-July 1913.

Left, bottom A generously scaled breakfast nook, illuminated by a large window, faces the garden.

Bridging a creek, this Berkeley house offers a wide balcony at its front for viewing the stream as it emerges from beneath the house. Sited toward the back of its lot to preserve the large front garden, the Dungan House is approached along a picturesque creek-side landscape. An old, magnificent, three-story-high wisteria frames the front door.

Architect John Hudson Thomas designed a remarkable group of houses during the prosperous years after the 1906 earthquake, largely in and around Berkeley. Thomas is best known for highly eclectic dwellings, often overscaled, even massive, and fairly bursting with architectural forms and imagery, much of it unexpected. In the Dungan House, a crowd of steep roofs meet at the front door. Dormers in different styles pierce the front roof, bringing light into the tall, wooden ceiling of the living room. The Dungan House's vividly styled, picturesque qualities are fully characteristic of Thomas's work.

The inspiration for this place, though, and possibly the concept for its site planning originated with Leo and Ella Dungan in concert with their close friend Bernard Maybeck. Though the house originally was clad entirely in shingles, a portion was later stuccoed in a half-timbered style, possibly after the 1923 fire, when Maybeck, who lost his own house along with many others he had designed, began to promote more fireproof construction. As with most buildings Maybeck influenced, the house has a very wide stair and is well arranged for performances and parties. Not coincidentally, Leo wrote plays in which Etta performed. When Leo became managing editor of the *Oakland Tribune*, the house became a venue for cultural and political events. According to grandson Michael Dungan, "Governors, artists, architects, Japanese spies, famous writers and educators have all passed time at the house."

As with many Brown Shingle architects, Thomas's work was little valued by the architectural community until relatively recently. According to local architect and historian Jim Stetson, Thomas's archive was offered to the architectural documents collection at Berkeley, his alma mater, but the university declined. Eventually, Thomas's papers and drawings went to the University of California, Santa Barbara, whose collection was established with a livelier, more inclusive vision by eminent California architectural historian David Gebhard.

167

The very tall, rustically finished, picturesquely fenestrated redwood board-and-
beam interior, anchored by a tall brick
fireplace, seems more a room at a Sierra
mountain camp than the living room of
a Berkeley house.

Opposite In the living room, with a view to the raised foyer and the dining room beyond, a notable feature is the built-in radio at the left of the stairs, particularly important to the very political life of this family (Mr. Dungan was the editor of the *Oakland Tribune*).

Above Contrasting with the radical asymmetries of the living room, the dining room is serene simplicity itself.

Left Hand-crafted, Japanese-inspired hardware at the front door prefigures the elegant paneling and casework detailing inside.

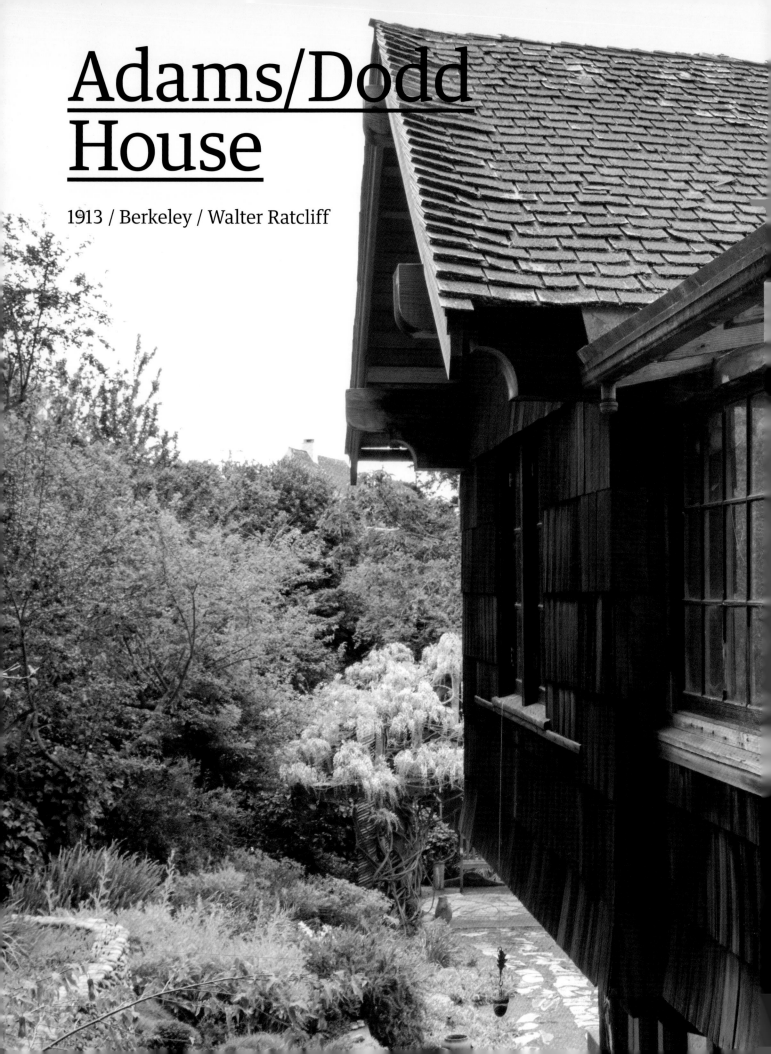

Adams/Dodd House

1913 / Berkeley / Walter Ratcliff

Previous pages Though much altered in the century since its construction, architect Walter Ratcliff's house for philosophy professor George Adams continues to focus on informal living, strong connections to the outdoors, and integration with the surrounding landscape.

Left Because Mrs. Adams was an avid gardener, the house includes a glazed conservatory along its southern facade, arranged, unusually, as part of the dining room.

Below, far left Wrapping around all sides of the house, the garden includes a playful gazebo constructed of spiral-wound steel sewer-pipe columns engulfed by an abundant wisteria.

Below, left Overscaled curved brackets support the projecting upper level, creating an ideal location for this fanciful, craftsman-style iron-and-glass lantern illuminating the entry stairs.

Englishman Walter Ratcliff, whose family moved to Berkeley when he was a teenager, is the only Brown Shingle architect whose firm continues into the twenty-first century. After graduating from Berkeley, Ratcliff trained in John Galen Howard's office, completing his architectural education in Paris and Rome. Returning to Berkeley, he designed more than a hundred houses in the boom years from 1908 to 1914, becoming the Berkeley City Architect in 1913. When Berkeley philosophy professor George Adams decided to move his family to the "country" north of campus, he asked Ratcliff for a dwelling on a site bordered only by a few farms. Mrs. Adams was a devoted gardener, and the house included a conservatory along the south side of the dining room, while the couple's bedroom above had views, in three directions, to the hills and bay.

Though no longer in the country, the house today retains a generous garden. Current owners have configured the garden with installations suggesting a late-twentieth-century version of bohemian life. A playful trellised gazebo is reached via a broken-ceramic-tile path, while walls encrusted with river rock and dinosaur bone lead to an orange-shaped produce stand dating from the 1950s and rescued from California's Central Valley—a funky version of Maybeck's idea that "Hillside Architecture is Landscape Gardening around a few rooms in case of rain."

177

Opposite Beyond the conservatory, the place's residents have designed the garden to include an artful set of curiosities. In the distance is a pop architecture icon, a 1950s orange juice stand in the shape and color of an orange, from California's Central Valley.

Above The dining room opens onto the south-facing conservatory.

Opposite, top The book-lined study provides wide views west to San Francisco Bay and toward the East Bay coastal mountains.

Right River rock-faced retaining walls support the uphill garden.

Opposite, bottom Like other Brown Shingle living rooms, the space is simply planned, redwood paneled, and focused on an overscaled brick fireplace.

The Igloo

1913 / San Anselmo / Matthew Bugbee

Shielded by dense vegetation from the nearby street and built atop a foundation of rough granite, this eccentric house by San Francisco architect Matthew Bugbee is an homage to the Alaskan Klondike.

Sitkum nika piah six.
—Translates to "Share my fire, friend"

In the house known as The Igloo, this motto, carved into the redwood header above the entrance to an indoor campfire nook, is rendered in the Chinook Jargon, a language developed between Native Americans and their European trading partners in the Pacific Northwest. Inuit totem poles flank steps down to the campfire from a tall living room designed to recall the Alaskan night sky, with small colored lights arranged on massive redwood timbers in imitation of the aurora borealis. For a different mood, huge hanging lanterns provide the colors of moonlight. The campfire room encircles a fireplace hood suspended over a pit designed for roasting meat. Redwood benches and bookcases line three sides, carved wooden Alaskan animal heads hold smaller lanterns in their teeth, and photographs of Klondike scenes, printed on glass windowpanes, filter light from outside.

This Brown Shingled house rests on a rustic stone base resembling a mountainous tumble of rocks. The front door is opened with a push on a bronze tree branch. Throughout, hardware and detailing include representations of some very wild animals—bedroom door knockers are shaped like bats, while bears and wolves hold campfire lanterns.

Almost entirely concealed by trees, The Igloo can easily be located by the adjacent eighty-five-foot-tall shingled water tower, the tallest of its type in the Bay Area. Originally, this tower housed a garage in its base, servants' quarters above, and a water tank and widow's walk at the highest level. Aside from being generally visionary, client George Breck was also an electrical wizard—at the time, only the most advanced houses were fully electric, and the elaborate lighting controls he installed here were far ahead of their time. (Breck was a "pioneer in photographic appliances and stage electrical lighting," according to his 1924 obituary.)

Matthew Bugbee, a third-generation San Francisco architect whose firm had built mansions for city scions, including Crockers, Floods, and the descendants of other early San Francisco magnates, built his own very unusual shingled home nearby. The architect was an enthusiastic partner in this idiosyncratic project, but it is clearly Breck's passion for Alaska which is at the place's heart.

Left The front-door hardware is cast in bronze as a rough-cut section of a tree.

Above The living room is realized as a very elegant barn, complete with gambrel form. Heavy beams are dotted with small colored lights designed to replicate the aurora borealis. Huge hanging lanterns may be switched to cast a dim, bluish light, a setting labeled "Moonlight Glow" on the elaborate early-twentieth-century lighting control panel.

SITKUM NIKA PIAH SIX.

186

Opposite Steps lead to the campfire pit and are flanked by Inuit totem poles. Carved across the header is a Chinook-language greeting.

Right, top A folkloric Alaskan creature, perhaps an otter, is one of four carved redwood animals holding lights in their mouths around the campfire. The lamp here features a bent cross, an ancient Eastern religious symbol.

Right, bottom At the campsite's center hangs a large wrought metal hood over a fireplace originally designed to roast meat. Built-in redwood seating wraps around three sides of the redwood-paneled room.

Postscript

1966 to the Present

James Hubbell's 1985 Sea Ranch Chapel on the Northern California coast, a landmark of organic architecture, takes maximum advantage of the vividly expressive, plastic possibilities of shingles.

"Back to Nature," a central slogan of the 1960s Bay Area counterculture, signaled, among other fresh directions, renewed interest in the natural world. As young people took to farms and communes to live simply and "close to the land," awareness of the fragility of the natural environment—especially California's redwood forests and Pacific coast—grew into advocacy for conservation. Environmental activists began campaigns to save the coast and old-growth redwoods, while their hippie counterparts challenged the status quo on every front. Social taboos were broken, with "free love" a new norm. Religious cults, ashrams, and gurus multiplied throughout California, while practices such as yoga and meditation became commonplace. Bay Area history was, of course, repeating itself. Young Bay Area hippies, subscribers to Jerry Rubin's advice, "Don't trust anyone over thirty," revived ideas espoused by their grandparents' generation. Bohemians at the turn of the century challenged social and architectural convention, possessed a profound reverence for nature, experimented with new religions and beliefs, and valued an artistic life over a more commercial one. With San Francisco's Beat poets of the 1950s and flower children of the 1960s, these ideas were reincarnated, again defining Northern California as a place on the nation's extreme edge, culturally as well as physically.

Architecture went back to nature too, and Brown Shingles enjoyed a renaissance in the 1960s. While

hippies built handmade cabins in the woods, the pioneering development at Sea Ranch, on the Northern California coast, captured the nation's architectural imagination. Referencing weathered wood vernacular buildings, particularly barns, and designed with shed roofs echoing the windswept nature of the site, the original buildings at Sea Ranch—the clustered dwellings and swim club by MLTW (Charles Moore, Donlyn Lyndon, William Turnbull, and Richard Whitaker), and the Sea Ranch Lodge and Hedgerow Houses by Joseph Esherick—were clad in either unpainted shingles or vertical redwood boards milled from locally felled trees.

Esherick's own house at Sea Ranch, a modernist cabin softened by its shingled sheathing, is an icon of the Third Bay Region Style. Ace Architects' 1993 Jordan Residence, built to replace the clients' house lost in the Oakland firestorm of 1991, recalls Maybeck's spectacular wood-shingled Hearst Hall (lost to an earlier Berkeley fire), with copper-clad shingles stretched across an eccentric form. Bart Prince's 1993 Hight House, north of Sea Ranch, reminds us of the remarkable plasticity and expressiveness of which shingles, the simplest of building materials, are capable. Essentially rustic yet refined, these latest Bay Area Brown Shingles, like their forebears, offer idiosyncratic and eclectic socially and historically resonant ideas about the particular act that is dwelling in Northern California.

Esherick Hedgerow House

1966 / Sea Ranch / Joseph Esherick

The central vision for the Sea Ranch: the land should remain primary, the buildings added to it should complement the essential character of the landscape that they would inhabit. The experience of the coastline was to be shared, not sequestered in separate private ownerships, and there would be large areas of commonly held land that would ensure the perpetuation of the coastal ecology.
—Donlyn Lyndon, The Sea Ranch (2004)

Joseph Esherick's firm, Esherick Homsey Dodge and Davis, together with MLTW, designed Sea Ranch's earliest buildings, setting in motion the vision described by Lyndon above. A group of small dwellings, the Hedgerow Demonstration Houses, formed a cluster nestled into windswept cypresses running toward the ocean. The houses were shed-roofed, angled to match the wind rake of the cypresses. They were Brown Shingles, with sod roofs.

Esherick, a meticulous craftsman who learned woodworking from his uncle, Wharton Esherick, the famed Pennsylvania craftsman, built the last of these houses for himself with his own hands. This dwelling is like a large piece of modernist furniture. George Homsey, his architectural partner, remembers that Esherick one day asked him to come over and help with construction (Homsey was building his own house nearby). Homsey declined, observing that Esherick was so demanding a carpenter that he might be impossible to assist.

Essentially, this house is a staircase, each room a landing. Its modernist wood detailing includes flush door and window casings, invisible cabinets, and windows arranged to dissolve the wall into the landscape beyond and to frame views as if they were paintings. Very small, in many ways quite perfect, Esherick's house is spare and efficient yet generously comfortable, even cosseting and serene, its occupants keenly aware, simultaneously, of the house and setting.

Architect Joseph Esherick's own house was among the first built at Sea Ranch. The original plan called for all houses there to be clustered together, as these are, and nestled into large cypress hedgerows and existing stands of redwoods, leaving the adjacent open meadows free of construction.

The modernist Stromberg House—built adjacent to the then sixty-year-old Van Sant House, designed by Ernest Coxhead, along Claremont Creek—reflects many of the same ideas about integrating the house with nature as its older neighbor, though rendered in different ways.

Stromberg House

1966 / Berkeley / Roger Lee

When modernist architect Roger Lee's Stromberg House was built in 1966 next door to Ernest Coxhead's 1906 Van Sant House, the neighbors were not happy. Yet today, this pair of houses seems elegantly contraposed, Brown Shingles from different eras, each designed to overlook the shared site and its creek—a kind of yin and yang of Bay Area domestic architecture. Roger Lee designed more than a hundred houses, primarily for middle-class clients like telephone-company employee Leonard Stromberg. Lee's work falls into the Second Bay Region Style, the modernist period when local architects adapted the tenets of the International Style to regional materials and living needs.

Paradoxically enough, the simple forms and volumes modernist houses require to be formally successful require a rigorous approach to structure and detailing. In Lee's sure hands, the language of modernism, an architecture of volume and light, planes and geometric solids, renders this house a sculpture responding delicately to its setting. With its cantilevered deck and projecting horizontal trellis, the new house appears to float over Claremont Creek.

Almost fifty years on, unaltered modernist works like the Stromberg House are increasingly rare. Clad in brown shingles, the house shows that modernism in the Bay Area can be a way to embrace nature, to dematerialize a building so that a surrounding natural setting is everything, the house itself something light, almost ephemeral, nearly disappearing.

Ace Architects designed this small, copper-shingled house for a woman publisher, one of the first to be built after the 1991 Oakland firestorm, as a fire-resistant homage to Maybeck's lost Hearst Hall, built by an earlier family in the publishing business and incinerated in an earlier devastating fire.

Jordan House

1993 / Oakland / Ace Architects

In October in the Bay Area, the anxiety begins. Indian Summer lingers, often bringing dry hot winds from the east rather than the usual ocean breezes, as well as a phenomenon known as "earthquake weather." Two years after the Loma Prieta earthquake struck the Bay Area in October 1989, the Oakland Hills firestorm of October 1991 destroyed thousands of houses. Halloween is enthusiastically celebrated in the Bay Area, in part because it marks October's end.

Dixie Jordan lost her 1920s Spanish Colonial-style Oakland home in the '91 fire. A journalist and publisher, Jordan was determined to rebuild a new dwelling for herself and her daughter. She recalled liking a controversial building in downtown Berkeley by Ace Architects, and she found the idea of creating an architecturally distinctive and colorful new home appealing.

Devastating fires regularly sweep through the region. Among the most notable of these earlier fires was the 1923 Berkeley fire, which destroyed a densely built neighborhood north of the university campus that was home to many Brown Shingles, including Hearst Hall, a women's gym commissioned by architecture patron and publishing heir Phoebe Hearst and designed by Bernard Maybeck. Its design featured a great, central Gothic-style room flanked by a pair of adjacent towers. Ace Architects designed the Jordan House as a miniature of the burned Hearst Hall, though with just a single tower and sheathed in copper-faced asphalt shingles rather than those cut from redwood trees. Over the front door is a redwood trellis, its beam ends shaped like dragons' heads, an homage to a signature Maybeck device.

Hight House

1993 / Mendocino / Bart Prince

In *The Shingle Style* (1955), Vincent Scully makes the case for the style's American roots. Bart Prince's Hight House, measured this way, might be called all-American. Trained by the American master of the improbable, the high-folk-art architect Bruce Goff, himself among the most extravagantly talented pupils of Frank Lloyd Wright, Prince's American design roots run deep. He is among that very small set of sophisticated practitioners whose work must be thought outsider architecture.

Mary Kay and Boyd Hight, an art history professor and her attorney husband, had long admired Prince's houses and asked that he design their vacation/retirement place near Mendocino, on the Northern California coast. Sixteen years on, they say, the house continues to surprise them. At first glance, the Hight House is baffling. Is it a building? And if so, is it a house?

Though bearing little resemblance to Brown Shingles of a hundred years ago, the Hight House shares many of their aspirations, especially the desire to merge the building with the natural environment through materials and considered siting. A shape-shifting brown-shingled wall stretches across a meadow, with a flap at one end suggesting an entry and a twist at the other revealing a wood-and-glass wall. Where older Brown Shingled roofs and walls bowed and flared, Prince's shingled roof/wall twists and undulates—a new order of plasticity that is nonetheless resonant with the antique Bay Area model developed in the late nineteenth century by inventive architects like Ernest Coxhead.

The structure undulates across a meadow along the Northern California coast, its geometries less conventionally architectural, more zoomorphic, and its extreme, sophisticated double curvature impossible to imagine in any material save simple redwood shingles.

Afterword

Survivors?

Top The Matteson House, a highly expressive, early-twentieth-century redwood-shingled dwelling cum Baha'i Temple: today, its exposed rafters, stacked corner beams, and extraordinarily eccentric wooden elements face multiple threats. Courtesy Jane Powell

Above The North Star House, a rustic Renaissance palazzo designed by Julia Morgan: though now on the National Register of Historic Places, this remarkable dwelling is much damaged, and its future is precarious. Courtesy North Star Historic Conservancy

Over time, Brown Shingles have fallen prey to wind, weather, and dry rot, fire, pests, and real estate development. More than a century has passed since Brown Shingles captured the imaginations of Bay Area avant-garde architects and their clients. While many remain standing, very few remain today as they were originally.

The places pictured in this volume are among these rare survivors—almost all diligently and affectionately maintained by owners fully aware of their roles in Bay Area architectural history. Sadly, there are many more houses bearing witness to neglect, indifference, contempt, and abuse—"progress."

The remarkable dwelling built by Jessie Matteson, a lumber mill owner, and his wife, Bernadette, in 1905, in the midst of fertile farmland, today is engulfed by later residential development in rough-and-ready East Oakland. Described by its current owner, architectural historian Jane Powell, as "Japo-Swiss," the house is planned around a U-shaped entry courtyard. Stacks of square-cut timbers form the corners in a style vaguely Scandinavian, reminscent of Matteson's Norwegian origins, while rafter tails at eaves and gable ends turn up with a Japan-esque flourish. Unique "nail head"-studded redwood paneling extends through the entry and ground floor, leading to

a living space that whips up Brown Shingle themes to an operatic pitch (the Mattesons were both musicians). Here, an inglenook literally surrounds the wildly picturesque freestanding clinker-brick fireplace, with a large part of the floor raised as a low stage. Matteson and his wife were leaders in establishing the Baha'i faith in the Bay Area, and this room provided the central meeting place for their congregation. Though Powell has long devoted her time, energy, and considerable expertise to the house's maintenance and restoration, the task ahead is considerable and daunting.

The North Star House in Grass Valley, designed by Julia Morgan in 1905, has endured considerably worse treatment. At the very center of California's Gold Rush Country, the North Star Mine was, at one time, the world's most productive gold mine. Engineer Arthur De Wint Foote became mine manager in 1895. Together with his wife, influential illustrator and writer Mary Hallock Foote, he commissioned this house, Julia Morgan's second residential work. The North Star House is rendered as a California version of a Renaissance Italian palazzo. The rusticated base is built of rough waste rock from the mining operations, a playful allusion to Florence's rusticated stonework. The lighter-appearing upper floor is also fashioned from materials taken from the site, with loggias and sleeping porches supported on tree trunks and walls clad in brown redwood shingles.

The house achieved notoriety with the 1972 publication of Wallace Stegner's Pulitzer Prize-winning novel *Angle of Repose*, based on Mary Hallock Foote's letters. (Though Stegner thanked the Foote family heirs in the book's opening pages, acknowledging that he had quoted from Mary's letters, the family and many academics were unhappy with Stegner's almost-but-not-quite-scandalous quotations and embellishments.)

The Foote family sold the place in the 1960s, and the house saw serial degradations, until at last it was scheduled for incineration as a fire department training exercise! With its destruction at hand, the small Grass Valley community rallied and eventually found the means to purchase the house. The North Star Historic Conservancy was formed, and the house was placed on the National Register of Historic Places in 2011. Derelict for years, the dwelling had suffered from a range of vandalisms, including trespassers tearing open its walls and fireplaces in vain searches for a rumored stash of gold. In its current, terribly vulnerable state, even with a small group of devoted volunteers, this important house barely clings to survival.

199

The Pied Piper of the Bay Region Style

John Beach with his wife, Mary Ann, in the 1960s.
Courtesy Deborah Loft

When we think of history, we think of events unfolding along an arc, a story, including passages perhaps improbable and, now, with hindsight's clarity, inevitable. We think of critical moments and crucial people, early indications, turning points, and eventual resolutions. Yet we almost never think of historians. Without historians, though, there is no history. Consider John Beach. Before him, there simply was no history of the first part of what, in 1947, *New Yorker* critic Lewis Mumford came to call the Bay Region Style. Beginning in the 1960s, and until his death from AIDS in 1985, Beach was the first to grasp the significances, understand the arcs and stories, of many of the most important early Bay Region architects, especially Ernest Coxhead, whose redwood-shingled conjures held Beach in special thrall. With long, diligent sleuthing, he uncovered, pieced together, and preserved Coxhead's archive.

Beach's work ranged widely, including studies of Bernard Maybeck and Julia Morgan, the best-known late-nineteenth- and early-twentieth-century Bay Area architects, as well as less familiar figures, whose intriguing, offbeat, always eclectic work might otherwise have been lost to history—John Hudson Thomas, Willis Polk, and several more, all of whose pivotal redwood-shingle houses form the core of this volume, which is dedicated to John.

201

For him, unlike other architectural historians of his time (and ours), there was no need of trotting out and polishing up an ideological agenda or his own political *bona fides*. Wonderful buildings were neither Marxian commodities nor inevitable consequences of the means of production. No, bigger game was afoot. Here is his description of Maybeck's Christian Science Church in Berkeley, from *Bay Area Houses* (1976):

It is prodigal enough of ideas to keep most architects busy for a lifetime. It is full of elegant makeshifts and sturdy sophistications. It is simultaneously Oriental, Gothic, Byzantine, and Californian. It is an open, welcoming gesture surrounding a quiet, private place. It is serene and flamboyant, enormous and unobtrusive. Its main space is defined by and glorifies its dramatically stated structural system (which the sensibilities of the 1950's applauded); yet the structure is largely coated with brilliant, intricate ornament (which the sensibilities of the 1950's opted simply to ignore). It poses hand-blown glass against catalogue factory sash and asbestos industrial paneling against hand-carved redwood architectural components. It has timber members which state structure with the clarity of a Miesian steel box, and

Romanesque capitals executed in reinforced concrete. It has high spaces and low, light spaces and dark, graceful elements and clumsy ones, simplicity and complexity— and wisteria which is as important as any of the purely architectural components.

John was unlike most architectural historians in other ways as well. There was the matter of his wardrobe. Among his characteristic costumes was one described as a muumuu, though this was not always patterned Hawaiian. More often, the shimmering rayon fabric printed with the range of modernist patterns put one in mind of the 1950s and 1960s. He often wore a simpler number, made (often by his mother) of two large squares of colorful, graphic polyester sewn together along the edges, with stitching omitted at the corners, allowing John's head, arms, and legs to pop through. I don't mention the other parts of his outfits because, often enough, there weren't any; and he much preferred to go without shoes.

In his appearance, Beach trod, usually barefoot, a path reaching back to Maybeck (whose very rustically tailored, homespun garb was much remarked upon), as well as other Northern Californian late-nineteenth- and early-twentieth-century signal idiosyncratic figures, including naturalist John Muir, Reverend Joseph Worcester, and painter William Keith. (A famous photograph of these men together reminds us of boxes of Smith Brothers cough drops.)

California has long imported many of its eccentrics, bohemians, and, later, Beatniks. Maybeck, Muir, Keith, and Worcester hailed from New York, Wisconsin, Scotland, and Massachusetts. John Beach was born in 1936 in Tahlequah, Oklahoma. As an adolescent, he undertook to visit architecture classes at the University of Oklahoma, in nearby Norman, making his way by bicycle. He befriended a professor there named Bruce Goff (the most fluorescently talented disciple of Frank Lloyd Wright). Goff loaned Beach his copy of Wright's Wasmuth Portfolio, and the game was on!

By the early 1960s, after a couple of years enrolled in Goff's classes at the University of Oklahoma and two more in the army (in Germany, maintaining nuclear weapons), Beach found his way to Los Angeles. With its relaxed way of life, Googie and more seriously modern architecture in full swing, and mile after mile of earlier unexplored, very often exotic buildings of every stylistic type, the place must have seemed a paradise to the nascent chronicler.

Beach fell in with architectural historians Esther McCoy and David Gebhard. For Gebhard, John worked on the earliest survey of the work of Los Angeles architect Rudolph Schindler, another Wright disciple. While interviewing the Lovells, for whom Schindler had designed a famous beach house, Mrs. Lovell is said to have remarked, "Rudy had affairs with all his clients' wives." Mr. Lovell's comments are not recorded.

In 1968, John married Mary Ann Beach, his future collaborator, at the Lloyd Wright-designed Wayfarers Chapel in Rancho Palos Verdes. That same year, they moved to Berkeley so that John might attend the architecture program at the University of California. He persevered for two years before the clash of his professor's International Style biases and John's bohemian eclecticism made continuing impossible.

In the meantime, Gebhard had given Beach an old photograph of a large, very idiosyncratic redwood-shingled church in San Francisco and asked him to get to the bottom of it. Once engaged, Beach was a dogged gumshoe, and he eventually identified this church as architect Ernest Coxhead's St. John the Evangelist, nicknamed "St. Roofus" in its day for its dominating, undulating, eccentric roofline. The building was destroyed in the 1906 earthquake. With his "discovery" of Coxhead, Beach's appetite was whetted, and in the following years he sleuthed out the architect's archive, literally rescuing his drawings, photographs, and memory from history's dustbin.

By the late 1960s and early 1970s, John was conducting architectural surveys, writing Bay Area architectural histories and guides, and, a favorite enterprise, leading tours and lectures. His talks were renowned for their passion, erudition, and the fact that many of his slides, frantically loaded into the projector only moments before, were sideways or even upside down. He was unconcerned, and the effect was very charming.

In 1975, architect Charles Moore, then teaching at UCLA, persuaded Beach to teach the school's course in Los Angeles architectural history, which continued, to the thrill of many and consternation of some, for three years. In the meantime, his marriage to Mary Ann, his collaborator on many inquiries, broke down. With this, some structure in his not-overstructured life was lost.

Yet by the first part of the 1980s, he was writing for *Architectural Digest*, a well-paying assignment his friends hoped might offer some mooring to a life increasingly at loose ends. In 1985, he returned from a writing assignment in Mexico, his familiar physical robustness much diminished. The late-arriving diagnosis was AIDS, and within a few months Beach was dead.

While at UCLA, Beach gave fellow architectural historian Charles Jencks a driving tour of Los Angeles. For the full effect, picture the spherical, Oklahoma-twanged, muu-muued Beach at the wheel, with the tall, slender, very dapper critic and scholar Jencks in the passenger seat. That ride led directly to Jencks's *Daydream Houses of Los Angeles* (1978). In the closely contested, publish-or-perish world of academe, indeed by any measure, Beach's tour that day was extraordinarily generous. When asked how he came to his encyclopedic knowledge of Bay Area and Los Angeles architecture, John freely and generously disclosed one of his secrets, offered up, unsurprisingly, as a driving tip: "Never make a U-turn if you can go around the block. Always take a different route coming than going."

Acknowledgments

*Most of us are mollusks after all, and are shaped
and sized by the walls we build around us.*
        —Charles Keeler, *The Simple Home*

Writers, artists, spiritualists and religious folk, schemers, visionaries, and other impractical people have long been drawn to the Bay Area. We have many of them to thank for embodying something of the spirit of Brown Shingle dwellings. Among these is Charles Keeler, whose 1904 *The Simple Home* is a manifesto setting out the ideas, patterns of living, and, especially, culture that provoked Brown Shingle architecture.

Other texts considering the period, establishing and defining the Bay Region Style, and documenting its ever diminishing architectural legacy include Sally Woodbridge's *Bay Area Houses* (1976)—which includes of particular note John Beach's "The Bay Region Tradition: 1890–1918"—Richard Longstreth's *On the Edge of the World: Four Architects in San Francisco at the Turn of the Century* (1983), and Leslie Freudenheim and Elizabeth Sussman's *Building with Nature: Roots of the San Francisco Bay Region Tradition* (1974). With a wider focus, Vincent Scully's *The Shingle Style and the Stick Style* (1955) was the first to consider the phenomenon of shingled architecture in America.

Berkeley is the epicenter of the Brown Shingle world, and the Berkeley Architectural Heritage Association has published a series of booklets documenting the city's neighborhoods, as well as organized annual walking tours over the past thirty-five years. Much of this effort is the work of historians Daniella Thompson and director Anthony Bruce, among others. The Berkeley Historical Society published *Berkeley Bohemia* (2008), a detailed record of the city in the late nineteenth and early twentieth centuries, written by Ed Herny, Shelley Rideout, and Katie Wadell. *The Guide to Architecture in Northern California and San Francisco* is an invaluable, Herculean achievement, first published in 1973. Here, David Gebhard, Sally and John Woodbridge, Robert Winter, and Roger Montgomery, with John and Mary Ann Beach and a host of other participants, researched, mapped, and described many of the region's notable buildings. A crowd of other well-written, well-researched works have expanded on these key texts, and many are included in our bibliography.

More recently, Paul Bockhorst's film *Designing with Nature: Arts and Crafts Architecture in Northern California* (2009) takes viewers on a remarkable tour through many of the period's signal buildings while at the same time recording a set of its most interesting historians.

Bay Area architectural historians are a particularly generous group, and we owe a debt to many of them. In addition to the authors and filmmaker mentioned above, we have received help and support from both professional historians and enthusiastic experts and amateurs, including Renee Aufort, Alice Carey, Judy Coy, Paul Duchscherer, Leslie Emmington, Paul Fisher, Daniel Gregory, Alan Hess, Peggy Levine, Gail Lombardi, Judith Lynch, Betty Marvin, Jane Powell, Jim Stetson, Bradley Wiedmaier, and Dave Weinstein.

Thank you, especially, to the homeowners who graciously rearranged their dwellings and schedules so that they might be included here: Anthony Bruce, Beverly Cheney and Avrum Gratch, Bruce and Joan Dodd, Michael and Betsy Dungan, Roger Erickson, Jim and Suzanne Friedman, Terry and Janet Geiser, Marilyn Gump, Anna and Michael Hearn, Boyd and Mary Kay Hight, Patsy Ishiyama, Dixie Jordan, Sharon Karol, Randy Knowles and Stephen Donwerth, Evelyn Larsen and Bill de Canon, Barbara Loomis and Stephen Elspas, Marlon Maus and Alan Selsor, Sarah Milne, Colleen Neff and Helmut Kapczynski, Anthony Newcomb, Ken and Susie Pope, Jane Powell, Carol Ann and Neilsen Rogers, the Sigma Phi fraternity, Barbara Trinkl, and Marissa Tweedie and Michael Brandon.

Our intrepid, patient photographer, David Livingston, climbed walls, leaned out windows, and precariously extended himself in many ways to gather the remarkable images that are at the heart of this book.

Our patient and supportive editors, David Morton, Douglas Curran, and Ron Broadhurst, suggested this book. Thanks to our old friend and classmate, Daniel Gregory, whose life is part of the Brown Shingle story; and to the book's designers, Alicia Cheng and Tom Wilder of MGMT. design.

And finally, thanks to our family and friends, especially Margaret Majua and our son, Max Howard, who, completely surprising us, read the rough manuscript and pronounced it "captivating," highest praise from our toughest critic.

Bibliography

Berkeley Architectural Heritage Association. A variety of booklets documenting Berkeley's neighborhoods and its architectural history, published since the organization was founded in 1974.

Cardwell, Kenneth H. *Bernard Maybeck: Artisan, Architect, Artist.* Santa Barbara and Salt Lake City: Peregrine Smith, 1977.

Freudenheim, Leslie, and Elizabeth Sussman. *Building with Nature: Roots of the San Francisco Bay Region Tradition.* Santa Barbara and Salt Lake City: Peregrine Smith, 1974.

Gebhard, David, Roger Montgomery, Robert Winter, John Woodbridge, and Sally Woodbridge. *A Guide to Architecture in San Francisco and Northern California.* Santa Barbara and Salt Lake City: Peregrine Smith, 1974.

Herny, Ed, Shelley Rideout, and Katie Wadell, *Berkeley Bohemia: Artists and Visionaries of the Early 20th Century.* Layton, Utah: Gibbs Smith, 2008.

Keeler, Charles. *The Simple Home.* San Francisco: Paul Elder, 1904.

Kostura, William. *Russian Hill: The Summit, 1853-1906.* San Francisco: Aerie Publications, 1997.

Longstreth, Richard. *On the Edge of the World: Four Architects in San Francisco at the Turn of the Century.* New York: Architectural History Foundation; Cambridge, Mass.: MIT Press, 1983.

Lyndon, Donlyn, and Jim Alinder. *The Sea Ranch.* New York: Princeton Architectural Press, 2004.

Maybeck, Bernard. *Palace of Fine Arts and Lagoon.* San Francisco: Paul Elder, 1915.

Olmsted, Roger, and T. H. Watkins. *Here Today: San Francisco's Architectural Heritage.* San Francisco: Chronicle, 1968.

Roth, Leland, with Bret Morgan. *Shingle Styles: Innovation and Tradition in American Architecture, 1874 to 1982.* New York: Harry N. Abrams, 1999.

Scully, Jr., Vincent. *The Shingle Style and the Stick Style: Architectural Theory and Design from Downing to the Origins of Wright.* 1955. Revised edition. New Haven and London: Yale University Press, 1971.

Scully, Vincent. *The Shingle Style Today or The Historian's Revenge.* New York: George Braziller, 1974.

Swift, Ann. *Cottages and Castles: The Centennial Houses of the City of Piedmont.* Piedmont, Calif.: The City of Piedmont, 2007.

Weingarten, David, and Alan Weintraub. *Bay Area Style: Houses of the San Francisco Bay Region.* New York: Rizzoli International Publications, 2004.

Weinstein, Dave. *It Came from Berkeley: How Berkeley Changed the World.* Layton, Utah: Gibbs Smith, 2008.

——. *Signature Architects of the San Francisco Bay Area.* Layton, Utah: Gibbs Smith, 2006.

Winter, Robert, ed. *Toward a Simpler Way of Life: The Arts and Crafts Architects of California.* Berkeley and Los Angeles: University of California Press, 1997.

Woodbridge, Sally, ed. *Bay Area Houses.* Salt Lake City: Peregrine Smith, 1976.

Woodbridge, Sally. *John Galen Howard and the University of California: The Design of a Great Public University Campus.* Berkeley and Los Angeles: University of California Press, 2002.

Woodbridge, Sally, and Richard Barnes. *Bernard Maybeck: Visionary Architect.* New York: Abbeville Press, 1992.

Worster, Donald. A *Passion for Nature: The Life of John Muir.* Oxford and New York: Oxford University Press, 2008.

Index

First published in the United States of America in 2013 by

Rizzoli International Publications, Inc.

300 Park Avenue South

New York, NY 10010

www.rizzoliusa.com

ISBN: 978-0-8478-4004-5

LCCN: 2012953992

Designed by MGMT. design

Distributed to the U.S. trade by Random House, New York

Printed and bound in China

2013 2014 2015 2016 2017 / 10 9 8 7 6 5 4 3 2 1